Death Is No Stranger

Helping Children Grieve

Cynthia Long Lasher

CSS Publishing Company, Inc., Lima, Ohio

DEATH IS NO STRANGER

Scripture quotations are from the New Revised Standard Version of the Bible, copyright 1989 by the Division of Christian Education of the National Council of the Churches of Christ in the USA. Used by permission.

Library of Congress Cataloging-in-Publication Data

Lasher, Cynthia Long.
    Death is no stranger : helping children grieve / Cynthia Long Lasher.
        p. cm.
    ISBN 0-7880-2505-8 (perfect bound : alk. paper)
    1. Bereavement in children—Religious aspects—Christianity. 2. Children and death—Religious aspects—Christianity. 3. Child rearing—Religious aspects—Christianity. I. Title.
    BV4596.P3L37 2008
    248.8'66—dc22

                                                                    2007037902

For more information about CSS Publishing Company resources, visit our website at www.csspub.com or email us at csr@csspub.com or call (800) 241-4056.

Cover design by Barbara Spencer
ISBN-13: 978-0-7880-2505-1
ISBN-10: 0-7880-2505-8   PRINTED IN USA

This book is dedicated to my late father. I wrote this after his diagnosis of lung cancer. He died 87 days later.

Each year at the Good Friday service, we sing that well-known hymn, "Were You There?" It is a hymn recalling the suffering death of Jesus Christ and God the Father's unconditional love for us. Ever since my baptism, I have known the love of my heavenly Father. Ever since March 3, 1965, I have known the love of my earthly father — you.

You Were There

You were there back in 1965 when God made me his child in the waters of Holy Baptism. How fortunate I was that you and Mom loved me so much that this precious and life-changing gift was given to me at such a young age!

You were there when I first learned to dribble the basketball and throw the discus and fall in love with the University of Virginia. Those years at basketball camp at UVA are some of my most precious memories from childhood!

You were there in the rain and cold as the other girls and I ran that eight-lap, two-mile race in high school. You remember, don't you — that event when I was so often lapped and the last runner to finish? Those are some of my most precious memories of you. I can see you there — hanging over the fence and cheering me on. I was never a loser in your eyes.

You were there to encourage me to go to Europe in high school and then to the Middle East in college. You gave me every opportunity to see the world and be exposed to other people and other cultures. I am the open-minded and inclusive person I am today because of opportunities like these that you made available to me.

You were there when that tornado took my best friend's life nearly fifteen years ago. You came to Alabama to support me and to help me make sense of the natural disaster and how it had affected my life. At every low point in my life, you were there.

Dad, you were there at every graduation and at *every* major turning point in my life.

I now find myself at a major turning point in your life. As your daughter, I want you to know — I have loved you my whole life, Dad. I am proud to be your daughter and to call you *my father*.

— Cynthia Long Lasher

Table Of Contents

Introduction

"Shhhhhh, shhhhhh, keep your voice down. I don't want the children to hear us talking about Grandma. They're too little to really understand. And, I don't think we should let them see us crying. So pull it together. Okay?"

While the adults in many families today are of the opinion that they should protect and shield children from death at any and all costs, in the long run, this approach to life and death can be very harmful to children. This book has been written to assist caring adults in helping children learn about death, and to provide information and guidelines on how adults might be able to help children to embrace their grief.

Before sharing some ways that caring adults might be able to help grieving children, it is important to define what grief is. Grief is how a person responds to loss. It is something people feel when someone we love or something we care about has been taken away from us. Children may grieve the loss of a pet, their old room, leaving their former school, or the death of their favorite elementary school teacher to cancer. For the purpose of this book, I will be addressing most specifically grief as it relates to the process that children go through when someone they love dies. Unlike the flu or the measles, grief is not an illness that can be treated medically and cured. Grief is a human process that must be experienced as a normal part of life. Just as people experience joy and excitement, we also express sadness and grief.

When it comes to talking with children about death and walking with them in their grief, there is no magical way of doing this. One of the best ways to help children experience healthy grieving is to model healthy grief ourselves. What is healthy grieving you might ask? Simply put, it is the complete opposite of the opening illustration given at the beginning of this chapter where family members insisted on shielding the children from Grandma's death.

Individuals who are healthy grievers are comfortable expressing their feelings openly with others. Healthy grievers will allow others to not only see feelings like sadness or depression, but will also not be afraid of expressing feelings such as anger and relief. To grieve in a healthy way means that hurting individuals are open to receive love and support from others. It also means being able to tell others what we need or do not need at any given point of the grief process.

When children witness adults crying or expressing their grief in a healthy way, this enables children to learn that it is okay for them to express their feelings as well. If children are taught that expressing feelings is not okay, then they will repress or stuff their feelings, which can be harmful in the future.

Children are members of our families and of our congregations. Therefore, they are very important people in our lives. Because we love and value them, they should not be forgotten or ignored when death touches their lives. Just as they need food, water, shelter, and security, so, too, do they need love and support when someone they love dies.

While there are manuals readily available on how to fix mechanical things and how to operate motor equipment and the like, a manual on how to "fix grieving children" is neither appropriate nor available. Because everyone grieves differently and because grief is a process that takes time and patience, no one book or pill can offer a quick fix. What grieving children need are caring adults who are willing to walk with them during their grief journeys. Walking with or companioning a grieving person involves listening, caring, and spending time with the grieving person.

Since there is no manual available on exactly how to enable others to grieve, most people learn how to do this by trial and error. By listening to children and interacting with them, children can teach us what it is like to be in a child's world. Only then will we be able to assist them in embracing their grief. As members of the Christian community, it is our responsibility and our privilege to walk with grieving children. Parents and relatives of grieving children cannot do this by themselves.

This book will provide its reader with information and some tips on how to educate children about death and how to support them when they are grieving. As people of faith, I invite you to be of the same mind as our Lord who spoke words of invitation to children. "Let the little children come to me, and do not stop them; for it is to such as these that the kingdom of heaven belongs" (Matthew 19:14).

Talking To Children About Death

Growing up in the Shenandoah Valley of Virginia, seeing dead animals along the road was a regular occurrence for me. Spotting a dead deer, skunk, or groundhog alongside the road was as familiar to me as a child as rush-hour traffic is to a person who commutes daily from Long Island into New York City.

Interacting with children informs us that children are not naive or unaware about death as some people might prefer to believe. Like me, many children have seen dead animals alongside the road or have had dogs, cats, gerbils, or some type of other family pets that have died. It would be quite unusual to talk to a child who has not had some type of exposure to death as a result of media coverage. Whether it comes from the television news report about the murder of a local family or the picture of an overturned car on the front page of the newspaper with the headlines, "Car crash kills two teens," most children are not immune from hearing or seeing death as part of their everyday lives. The death of a beloved pet, a tragic loss of a teenager to an automobile accident, or even the change of seasons, provide caring adults with "teachable moments."

"Teachable moments" are opportunities for adults to teach children about life and death. When children are able to have some previous exposure to death before someone close to them dies, this can be of great benefit to them. Instead of postponing talking about death with children until someone they love dies, I would encourage caring adults to take advantage of "teachable moments" prior to your child's first death experience.

It does not take long for children to understand that flowers bloom and then later die. From life experiences, many children learn that the flowers they gave to their mothers for Mother's Day died after a few weeks and had to be thrown into the trash. Goldfish and basset hounds will not live forever, either. Children learn by playing with Barney, the basset hound, that he is getting old and cannot play as long as he used to. Likewise, Grandma and Grandpa are getting old and slowing down, as well.

11

Talking to children about death as a natural part of life will make the death of a parent, a grandparent, or a close friend easier to confront. Adults need to help children understand that death is a part of life. Just as babies are born with each new day, simultaneously, people are dying. Life is full of both beginnings and endings. As adults who love and care for children, it is our responsibility to help our children learn about both life and death just as it is our responsibility to feed, clothe, and send our children to school.

We are teachers and role models for our children. When I speak about "our" children, I am not only referring to parents and guardians. I am addressing the whole church family who together are responsible for providing spiritual and emotional care for children who are in our congregations and our neighborhoods. As role models and teachers, if we model that death is not a normal part of life, then our children will grow up denying that death will ever touch their lives.

When the leaves change in the fall, use that opportunity to talk about the cycle of life. When the pet rabbit dies, do not rush to the pet store and secretly replace Bunny. Talk to the child about the rabbit's death and invite the child to help you bury the rabbit. Some parents have discovered that taking a child to the funeral of an acquaintance may be a helpful experience. While not being extremely close to the person who died, the funeral will provide the child with some exposure of what takes place at a funeral. By doing this, the child will have already some experience with what happens at funerals before having to attend a funeral for someone loved.

Children are much smarter than most adults realize. While adults are huddling around the coffeepot in the kitchen whispering about the details of Daphne's death, it is not uncommon for little Sally to be listening from the next room. The more adults try to keep things from the children, the more confusing and frightening death is for children. In cases where the details about the cause of death are hard for adults to accept, such as suicide or murder, some individuals have tried to withhold this painful information from their children. While their efforts are certainly understandable and commendable, in many cases this has backfired.

Telling your teenage daughter that Uncle Gus died by a bad fall instead of telling her that it was actually suicide might lend itself to her feeling distrust and anger toward her family. Not only do children listen in on adult conversations when adults do not know that they are listening, but some children look through their family's papers when no one is around. I have talked to children who found out the real cause of death by discovering the death certificate in a folder or file cabinet.

Be honest with children as much as possible. While children do not always need to know every fact and detail, the truth is often more helpful than creating lies that are hard to perpetuate. Resentment, anger, and distrust will most likely surface if a child finds out that outright lies were told to him or her. If at all possible, remember that honesty is always the best policy. Keeping secrets and hiding the truth backfires more often that it protects. Also, ask yourself who is being protected by not telling the truth. Are you really trying to protect the children, or is keeping the secret being done to make things easier for you?

When children are not given complete or accurate information about the death of a loved one, they often utilize what is called "magical thinking." Children have very creative minds and vivid imaginations. When information is withheld from children or when adults are secretive, some children will create an image of what might have happened to their loved one, which could be more painful or graphic than the truth. Children who exhibit magical thinking also are prone to blame themselves for things because they think their thoughts and their wishes have the power to control events and circumstances.

When talking to children about the cause of death and details of it, speak to them at their developmental level. Explaining how Max died from the car accident should be told to a six-year-old differently from how you would tell a teenager. Offer a simple, yet truthful, explanation. Then wait for their questions. Do not project your feelings or your anxieties about the cause of death to the children. How they hear the details may be very different from how you heard the details. When telling children about a death, it is sometimes helpful to talk to the children separately if the difference in age between your children is more than two or three years. What is told to a ten-year-old should be different from what is told to a five-year-old.

Answer their questions as truthfully as you can while simultaneously keeping in mind their age, their cognitive abilities, and their prior experiences with death. If you do not know the answer to their questions, then be truthful about that. Children need to be told that sometimes adults do not always understand everything, either. Sometimes life just does not make sense, and sometimes life does not seem fair. Hearing that from an adult can be very beneficial to children when they are struggling to make sense of things.

Sometimes, children do not want or need to know every detail; rather, they need assurance that you will not be leaving them. When loved ones die, small children have anxiety about being abandoned. Be mindful that while you, as the adult, might be preoccupied with the cause of death or working out the details for the funeral, grieving children might be more fearful about losing you or worrying about what will happen to them in the future.

Sometimes when a parent dies and he or she was the source of the family's income, children worry about having to move out of their home or change schools. While this might sound self-centered to most adults, children are very egocentric in their thinking. Instead of being caught up in all the details of the death like their mother and older sister, Johnny and Joey might be more worried about their home being sold and changing schools rather than being preoccupied with the when, where, and how of their father's death.

Regarding the best time to tell children difficult information, the best rule of thumb is to tell the children as soon as possible after the death or loss has occurred. Tell them the truth, but on their developmental level, then listen carefully for their questions and concerns. Do not overwhelm them with details if they do not ask for them. On the other hand, let them know that they can always talk to you. Touch base with them a little every day to keep the communication lines open. A few days may go by before they want to talk about anything specific. That is normal and okay. Children can only absorb a limited amount of painful information at one time.

When talking to children about death, avoid euphemisms at all times. This next point is one that I hope readers will take from this book: In most cases, euphemisms cause more pain and harm than good! Rarely in my fifteen years of ministry and working with grieving individuals have I ever heard someone say that a euphemism made them feel better. On the other hand, countless numbers of people have expressed to me the hurt and pain they felt when someone spoke a well-intended euphemism to them. Like adults, children do not need to hear words from people that might cause them any additional pain.

What are these euphemisms you might be asking yourself? Euphemisms are familiar and overly used expressions that people often speak when they are at a loss for words. They are "slang expressions" that have become commonplace in the English language. Examples of euphemisms include the following:

- God doesn't give us more than we can handle.
- You are lucky. You still have two other sisters to play with.
- What God brings us to, God gets us through.
- Be strong. Big boys don't cry.
- If you look around, you will see that someone else is worse off than us.
- You're young. You can bounce back from this.
- Get yourself together. Others are looking to you for strength.

Reflect upon this illustration and ask yourself how Brianna might have felt when her best friend's mother attempted to comfort the eleven-year-old girl two weeks after her brother died from SIDS. One Sunday morning as Brianna was walking down the hall following Sunday school, Katie's mother came up to her and embraced Brianna in her arms. As Brianna began to sob, Katie's mother was at a loss for words. Feeling that she needed to say something, she remembered a euphemism that she had heard many times. With her left arm around Brianna, she spoke these words: "God needed another angel in heaven. Baby Mickey is with God now."

Later that night, Brianna asked her mother as she was tucking her into bed, "Did God really take Baby Mickey because he needed him to be an angel in heaven? Why did God have to take our Mickey, Mommy?" Brianna began to cry as her mother reached down to hold her sobbing daughter. Even though Katie's mother certainly did not mean to cause Brianna additional pain, her words not only caused pain but also raised questions about her faith in a loving God.

Many children are sensitive like Brianna. Children are also inquisitive by nature. They ask lots of questions and notice more things than adults give them credit for. When a funeral procession passes by their house or when the pastor announces at worship that a church member has died, small children often ask their parents, "Who is dead? What happens when someone dies?"

For parents and adults who raise children, these are some of the most difficult questions to answer. Every child is different and no two children are alike in how they will understand death, therefore, the best way to talk about death is to use simple language. One of the best ways to describe death to children is to talk about what happens to the human body when someone dies.

When someone dies, the body is no longer physically alive. When people die, they no longer breathe. When people die, their hearts stop beating. Instead of focusing on the emotional aspects of death like missing the person or no longer having them around to talk to, focus on what physically happens to a person's body upon death. A person who has died cannot hear, speak, or smell anymore. A person who has died no longer experiences pain.

As harsh as it might sound, use the words "dead" and "die" with children. People sometimes try to soften their words by using euphemisms. Euphemisms often confuse children. They can also make children fearful of being abandoned or afraid to go to sleep. Once again, I recommend that you avoid using euphemisms. Some of the most common euphemisms that people use to describe death include the following:

- passed away in his or her sleep,
- passed on,
- is sleeping,
- left us,
- went home, or
- is no longer with us.

Instead of using these or other euphemisms, use everyday examples of death when talking with children. Remind them of the summer day when they found the dead squirrel in the park. Do they remember that the squirrel was not breathing anymore? The squirrel's body was still and quiet. You can then talk about the fact that the dead squirrel would never run or move again. No longer would the squirrel need to frantically search for food or water because its body was no longer alive. Its body was at peace.

When seasons change, this can provide another teaching opportunity for caring adults. This is a wonderful way to explain how death is a part of life. As leaves fall from trees and die, children can be taught that change and death are part of life. When raking the leaves in the yard, use this as a time for sharing about life and death.

Young children are literal thinkers. They take the words of adults to be literal truths. If they accompany you to the funeral home upon a neighbor's death and you inform them that their neighbor is "sleeping," your children may be afraid to go to sleep that night. The same is true for using the language of "taking a trip." When told that a dead person is "gone away" or "on a trip," children might later become frightened and anxious when you go out of town for several days. An honest and truthful approach works best with children. Like adults, children value honesty and sincerity.

Relating To Children After They Have Been Affected By Death

Pablo was the typical overachieving little boy throughout elementary school. He was one of the most popular students in his class. "Funny, smart, and good at sports" is how his friend once described him. However, when Pablo's father was killed at work, due to a mistake by a coworker, everything changed for Pablo. Not only did his grades drop in school and his interest in sports and friends fall off, but Pablo began to fall into a deep depression.

Being an only child, Pablo was the apple of his father's eye. Even though he had begun middle school, Pablo's father remained the boy's confidant. There were never any secrets between the son and his father. Whenever the two finished a game of basketball, they never just "high-fived," rather, they always hugged one another. Pablo's father was often commended for not being afraid of showing his love for his son in public. Many Sundays after receiving holy communion at Trinity Church, Pablo's father would walk down the center aisle of the nave with his arm draped around his son's shoulder.

When Pablo's father died, neighbors described Pablo's functioning as if "all the wind has been swept out of Pablo's sails." Pablo continued to cry himself to sleep at night for months after his father's death. He withdrew from friends and extracurricular activities at school and lost fifteen pounds in three months. Instead of expressing his feelings to his mother or to his friends, he shut down emotionally and physically.

While his mother and other relatives were focused on learning all the details that surrounded the accident, Pablo was not interested in those details. Pablo missed the emotional support he had always received from his father. The middle-school student also experienced many secondary losses such as the loss of his confidant, his basketball partner, and his hero.

When reflecting upon Pablo's story and his grief, there are things that adults can learn from this grieving boy. The first point is to acknowledge that everyone grieves differently. While his mother and many of his relatives were giving a great deal of energy to learning more about the cause of death, for Pablo this was not as important. Missing the emotional support and grieving the relationship with his father were key losses for Pablo.

Sometimes children feel alone in their grief when they recognize that others are grieving differently than they. In Pablo's case, he resented the fact that others were preoccupied with finding facts while he was feeling alone in his sadness and depression. Some children feel abandoned when one parent dies and the surviving parent is unable to meet their emotional needs. While the surviving parent may be personally grieving so much that he or she is unable to provide support for his or her children, in other cases the surviving parent may simply not know what to do to help others who are hurting.

In situations like Pablo's, the support and the compassionate presence of church members and caring adults can be of great benefit. Recognizing that others care and are willing to walk with you when you are grieving makes many grieving people feel less alone. In Matthew's gospel there are many quotations on humility and forgiveness. Jesus spoke these words, "Where two or three are gathered in my name, I am there among them" (Matthew 18:20). As God's people, I would exhort you to be aware of "windows of opportunities" like this to extend God's grace to others.

Upon learning about the death of a loved one, family members have to make a number of important decisions within a short period of time. Not only do decisions have to be made about when and where to hold the funeral or memorial service, but a number of decisions have to be made regarding children as well. Parents and relatives need to come to an agreement on how to tell the children about the death, and they need to make a decision about whether or not their children will be allowed to attend the funeral. For the sake of simplicity, I will use the term "funeral" throughout this book to refer to the service where the loved one is remembered and honored. In some cases, the service may be a memorial service or a

20

"celebration of life service"; however, for the purpose of this book I will refer to this event as the "funeral."

Making decisions about your children attending the viewing and the funeral is a personal decision. Every family must make this decision on their own. As a minister and a grief specialist, I am frequently asked my thoughts on this subject. Henceforth, what I write in this chapter is based on my personal experience of having walked with grieving individuals and on what I have read and learned from others who work in the field of grief and loss.

Most experts on children agree that children should be included in all aspects of the grieving process, including the funeral. Developmentally, children are not able to comprehend that death is final until around five or six years old, however, children should not be excluded from this family ritual. The importance of being included in a key family event is more important for small children than is their ability to understand what has happened. On the other hand, if children are excluded and left at home, they will use their imaginations to fantasize and imagine what is going on at the funeral and with their loved one's body.

Before taking children to the viewing and funeral, they should first be asked if they want to attend. Adults should not force children to attend if they do not want to, nor should adults assume that they are too little to understand. Most children are smarter than we give them credit for. Nevertheless, we as caring adults are responsible for helping them understand what to expect once they arrive at the funeral home or church. Spending time talking about the funeral and the viewing, and being open to a whole gamut of questions is essential, if healthy grieving is the desired goal.

Regarding the viewing, children generally want to see and often touch the body. This should not be forced by adults. Let children do what they are comfortable with. Before viewing the body, children should be informed that what they will see at the funeral home is merely the physical body of the person. That person no longer breathes. She can no longer hear them talking, and she will never get hungry or thirsty again. If she had experienced pain prior to death, inform the children that she no longer has pain. It should be explained that death is not a punishment nor is it something to be afraid of. Just as there is a time when we were born, there is also a time when we must die.

Explaining what to expect at the funeral is also very important. Funerals are a time when friends and loved ones gather to remember the person who died, and it is a time to say, "Good-bye." At the funeral of a Christian, other believers gather to hear God's words of comfort and hope. At most funerals, Christians are reminded that our loved one's death is not the end, rather, that this believer has been brought into a new relationship with God.

At a Christian funeral, the pastor will speak to assure those present that nothing can separate us from God's love. Not even death can separate us from God. While we will surely miss our loved one, at the same time we know that we are not alone in our grief. The funeral is a time for public mourning as well as a time for Christians to share together God's love for his children.

Following the death of a loved one, it is important to encourage children to remember their loved ones. Talking about their loved ones and sharing stories is very therapeutic and healing. Remembering the time Grandpa slipped and fell into the creek, or the time he came to watch your graduation from elementary school and got caught in the rainstorm, will help a grieving grandchild feel less alone in his grief. Sometimes relatives or friends are afraid to mention the departed loved one for fear of tears or sadness.

My experience indicates that it is much better to have others remember our loved ones, which might make us cry, than it is to never mention their names in public again. No one wants to think that somehow their loved one has been forgotten. That is very painful. It is generally better to err on the side of recalling a loved one, rather than never mentioning their name again. Listening to stories and recalling times spent together is often received with openness and gratitude.

While we will never see our loved one again, we can always treasure our memories. My late father repeatedly told me, "What you have learned in life and what you have experienced no one can take from you. People can take away your money and your possessions, but they cannot take away what you have learned."

Dying does not mean that we forget our loved ones, but it does mean that we will never be able to see them laugh again or hear their funny jokes again. A good way for children to keep their memories alive is to encourage them to keep a "memory box" with special things in it that reminds them of their loved one. Also, creating a "memory book" with special pictures, drawings, a good-bye letter, and so on, may help grieving children come to grips with the finality of death. Later in life, these mementos will help the loved ones remember the person who died.

Parents and caring adults need to always keep the communication door open to grieving children. Children should never be scolded for asking questions, even if it is a question that has been asked before. When children are grieving and trying to "make sense of" a death, they often ask the same question over and over again. While this might be annoying to adults, this is a normal part of the grieving process. By asking questions, people are able to move through their grief.

While children might not have many questions upon first learning about a death, in the months and years that follow, questions might arise. As children mature in their thinking, they may ask questions that they were not capable of conjecturing when they first learned about the death. People often "re-grieve" death at different points in their lives. This means that as people age and experience life, they may encounter new and different grief reactions in response to a specific life event or circumstance.

For example, if Benji's twin brother died when he was a toddler, he was not capable of asking a lot of questions about Benji's death. However when Benji graduates from junior high or goes to his first prom, he may miss not having his brother to share these experiences with him. He may also ask detailed questions about how his brother died, and he may want to look at scrapbooks from his childhood at a time when most of his friends are busy having fun and looking toward their futures. Encouraging dialogue and open communication is a must for healthy grieving! When Benji discovers that his parents and his church family are more than willing to talk about his twin brother and to answer his questions, he will be much more able to resolve his grief and cope with other losses in the future.

As children enter school and get involved in groups and activities within the community, the people they know and relate to in these groups become increasingly important to them. When a death happens that affects children, it is imperative that the leaders and administrators of schools, clubs, and after-care programs be informed about the death as soon as possible. Anyone who has daily contact with children should be told about the death so that they might be prepared to walk with children through their grief journeys. Sometimes it is the school bus driver or the coach who will be the person who can provide support and empathy when children are feeling vulnerable and broken. Teachers especially need to be informed so that they will better understand grief reactions in the classroom.

In one of my congregations, eight-year-old Ivan had a very difficult time with his grandfather's death. Returning to school several days after the funeral, Ivan began to cry one afternoon during recess. Because his teacher knew about the death of his grandfather, the caring and observant teacher called Ivan's parents to inform them about Ivan's behavior. Upon noticing this and other behavioral changes, Ivan's mother initiated contact with me and Ivan and I began some play therapy. During our time together, I discovered that Ivan needed permission to express his sadness over missing his grandfather. Due to a caring teacher and nurturing parents, Ivan was able to work through this initial stage of his grieving.

Thomas Merton wrote in his book, *No Man Is An Island*, that "true happiness is found in an unselfish love, a love that increases in proportion as it is shared." As people of faith, Christians do not live as isolated individuals. Instead, Christians live in community. One of the great benefits of being a Christian is that we do not have to experience hardship or grief by ourselves. Children have a great deal to teach adults about grief and how it affects them. When we, as caring adults, open ourselves up to their teaching and their love, we may discover that both they and we benefit and grow.

Factors That Influence How Children May Respond To Death

Debbie and Kay sat looking at each other in shock when they discovered that both of them had lost their fathers in car accidents two years prior. While playing together on a summer soccer league in the neighborhood, neither girl realized that her teammate had also lost her father to death. As the girls participated in a newly started support group at their middle school, they were learning a number of new things about one another. Even though the car accidents were similar in some ways and both of their fathers had died suddenly, how the girls each responded to the deaths were quite different.

Being extremely close to her father, the death of Debbie's dad devastated her. Debbie recalled crying herself to sleep for months after her father's accident. She also talked about how she lost a lot of weight after his death and how she lost interest in soccer and school for about six months. As Kay talked about her father, feelings of anger surfaced. Kay's father had been physically abusive to her mother and to her older sister for most of Kay's childhood.

Stories of her father hitting her mother began to flow from Kay's mouth when the group facilitator asked Kay to describe her father. After recalling several incidents about his abusive behavior, Kay went on to inform the group that her mother finally divorced her father about three years prior to his death. Not long after moving out of the house, her father quickly found a girlfriend and wanted nothing to do with Kay and her older sister, Allison.

At one point in the group, Kay looked to Debbie and said to her, "I'm sorry to hear about your dad's death. Your dad sounded like a great father. My dad was a jerk. I don't miss him at all. Actually, I am kind of relieved that he is dead. I don't ever have to worry about his hurting Mom or Allison again. While he never hit me, he threatened me a couple of times. Allison and I went to his funeral, but neither of us cried. You know, Dad never once told me that he loved me. He once told me that using mushy words like that was for sissies."

There are many factors that influence how a child will respond to the death of a relative or loved one. The story of Debbie and Kay illustrates that while two stories might sound similar in some ways, how children grieve the death of someone varies greatly. While the cause of death and the time of death were very compatible, how the two girls responded to the deaths of their fathers was completely different.

While every situation is unique, there are a number of factors that need to be remembered when death touches the lives of children. Perhaps the most significant factor, which influences how children respond to the death of a relative or loved one, is the relationship that the child had with the deceased. Here are a few questions that caring adults may want to ask themselves upon learning that a child they care about has lost someone in his or her family or inner circle. "Was the child emotionally attached and close to the person that died?" or "Was the relationship strained, unresolved, or complicated, or was the relationship somewhere in between?"

When children lose people who were significant in their everyday lives, the loss is generally much more difficult than when the person who died was more removed from their lives. For example, if a school-age girl loses a grandmother who lived next door and helped to raise her, this will most likely be more difficult to bear than losing her other grandmother who lived across the county, and only saw her granddaughter three times in the child's life. When people that children have spent a lot of time with or had a strong and loving relationship with die, the absence of this person in their lives often impacts grieving children more than it would when the relationship was less close.

When divorced, abusive, or blended families are involved, never assume that you know how a child thinks or feels. Instead, invite and allow the grieving child to teach you about the relationship. Let grieving children know that even if the relationship was not good, that you are there to help them process their feelings and embrace their grief — whatever that means for them.

If the person who died was a relative who was estranged or unknown to the child, be aware that the child may grieve the fact that with the death there is no possibility for a future relationship or reconciliation. Keep in mind that grief reactions can include a variety of feelings beyond those that are most familiar like sadness, loneliness, and anger. A sometimes-forgotten grief reaction might include the loss of hope or dreams. The death of a person may end any hope of one day "having the daddy or mommy I always dreamed of."

When the person who died had been physically, emotionally, or sexually abusive to the child or to someone that he or she loved, this also influences how the child will view the death. Sometimes relief is felt by the children. Other times, children may feel guilt or anger. Instead of projecting what you think you might feel if you "were in their shoes," invite the grieving child to find a way to express their innermost thoughts and feelings. Never put words into their mouths by saying things like: "I bet you are feeling such and such since your stepfather died, aren't you?" Instead you might want to be truthful and state, "I have no idea what this must be like for you. Things sound kind of complicated. I want you to know that I am here if you ever want to talk."

How a person died is another key factor that influences how children grieve a death. Was the death as a result of a suicide, a drunk-driving incident, a drug overdose, a murder, a terrorist attack, or some other type of violent death? These are all examples of a sudden death or deaths "without warning." Other examples of sudden death include a heart attack, an aneurysm, a work-related death, a sports-related death, a drowning, and so on.

Others may die from a death that has been anticipated. Examples of anticipatory deaths would include a death from a terminal illness, a chronic illness, or a lingering death as a result of an accident where there was little hope for recovery. Some types of anticipated death include cancer, AIDS, leukemia, Lou Gehrig's disease, and so on.

If children have personally witnessed the death, this can have a big impact on how children embrace their grief and cope with the loss. In cases of violent or sudden death, witnessing a death can be traumatic. Professional help may be needed in some of these cases. Watching a loved one die in pain can also be devastating to some children. When a child uses words like, "She just lingered" or "I couldn't stand to see him suffer," this is an indication that witnessing the death was quite difficult for the child.

Listen to what grieving children are telling you. Ask them to tell you what they remembered the most about the death or what was the most difficult for them. You may want to ask them to talk about their understanding of the person's death. If children are too young to verbalize their thoughts and feelings, encourage them to draw a picture or express themselves through some type of play or art. An observant adult will quickly discover that children internalize and think more deeply about things than some of us realize.

There are stigmas attached to certain types of deaths in every culture. In America, some people associate death by AIDS or suicide as being shameful or embarrassing to surviving family members and loved ones. When I was in high school, one of my cousins died. He was in his twenties. At the time, we were told that Matt had died from cancer. Later on, I learned that Matt was gay and had died from AIDS. In time, I learned that my relatives were uncomfortable with Matt's homosexual orientation and therefore chose to keep the truth from most of the people in our community.

When a person completes suicide, family members have to decide how to handle informing people of the cause of death. In many instances, family members will either avoid disclosing the cause of death, or will often distort the truth for fear of public embarrassment or shame. When children are told the truth about the cause of death in cases such as suicide, AIDS, and the like, it is imperative that the adults around them help them understand that nothing can change or remove the love they had for their loved one. Hurtful comments or judgmental statements by others may be painful to hear, but children should be reminded that their memories and their feelings for their loved one are theirs to keep and to treasure.

Previous experience or lack of experience with loss will affect how death affects children. If children have never experienced the death of someone close to them before and their life has been relatively free from major losses and changes such as divorce, moving, changing schools, and so on, the first death of a loved one may be especially difficult and traumatic for them. On the other hand, when children have had some previous exposure to death, such as a death of an elderly neighbor or a distant relative where the child was permitted to attend the funeral and was included in the public mourning process, this sometimes makes the death of someone loved a little bit easier. Children who have been sheltered from death and other types of loss often find the death of someone close to them more painful and confusing.

When children have been exposed to death and have been encouraged to participate in the rituals surrounding it such as attending the funeral, visiting the family's home and delivering a meal, and signing their name to a sympathy card, this provides them with some exposure to grief before their first personal and close encounter with it themselves. Likewise, when children have experienced the divorce of their parents and have firsthand experience of the myriad of losses that accompany divorce, this will most likely influence how they adjust and respond to the death of a loved one.

Like adults, children learn from life experiences. The death of a pet or the death of a beloved pastor or teacher will influence how children handle and embrace the death of a relative or close friend. While no two deaths or no two relationships are alike or truly comparable, previous experience can play a big role in how children confront the death of someone loved.

One's culture also affects how children will respond to the death of a loved one. Because every culture is different in how they view death and the afterlife, the cultural beliefs of a family will have a direct impact on children. While some cultures embrace death more openly than others, how the adults around them understand death will influence the children.

The age of children has a big influence on how they will respond to the death of someone they loved. While this topic will be covered in depth in an upcoming chapter, it is important to mention here that even small children are capable of responding to the death of someone loved. Even though infants and toddlers are not able to understand the permanence of death, they are capable of sensing the emotions of others around them when death touches the life of their family.

When the captain and the chaplain of the police department arrived at the Brandts' house to inform them that their father had been killed in the line of duty, the emotional outburst of the family's two-year-old meant something very different than the crying and screaming of the nine-year-old. As everyone erupted into tears upon hearing the details of the death, the youngest family member was not immune from the tragic news. While unable to comprehend the news, the two-year-old was sensitive enough to realize that something has happened to disrupt the family's equilibrium.

Not only does the age of children influence how they will respond to the death of someone loved, but their maturity and life experience will also play a key role. Also the physical, mental, and spiritual strength of children can either assist or hinder children in how they embrace and accept the death. For example, a mature fourteen-year-old girl who helps to take care of her younger siblings because her mother is an alcoholic and her father abandoned the family five years ago, will respond to the terminal illness and death of her older sister differently than would an immature fourteen-year-old girl who is pampered.

When children have mental limitations, such as mental retardation or Down syndrome, this will affect how they deal with death. Likewise, children who have been encouraged to go outside to exercise or play when life has been challenging for them, will embrace death differently than children who have been taught that watching movies or videos and indulging in ice cream, will make all their problems disappear. Having a spiritual foundation or a belief in the afterlife will also influence how children embrace death as opposed to children who have been taught that physical death is the end of one's existence.

When children are brought up in homes or in communities where a faith tradition is a big part of their sense of belonging and their sense of meaning, this generally affects how death is understood and accepted by children. Even though some children will become angry and may even rebel at God when someone loved has died, having some type of religious foundation or a strong sense of spirituality often helps children to make some sense of the loss provided a period of time has elapsed. In homes where religion or spirituality is downplayed or even discouraged, this can often become a hindrance to children when tragedy and crisis enters their lives.

Adults are not the only people in life who "search for meaning" and try to make sense out of things when death or bad things happen in life. Children also ask the familiar "Why?" question. When brought up in families or in faith communities where asking this question is not discouraged nor put down, children often learn that it is okay to question God's presence or God's role in the events of everyday life. Asking questions and searching for meaning does not mean a lack of faith; rather, it usually indicates the faith of a believer who is merely struggling to make sense of out something painful or confusing.

How the adults around them are coping and embracing the death has a big influence on grieving children. When children are allowed to participate in the family's mourning process, as opposed to being protected or excluded from it, this can have a very powerful and positive impact on children. When families choose to keep the communication lines open with their children, and when adults model that it is okay to express feelings like anger, confusion, sadness, and so on, this shows children that grief is a normal part of life.

Daddy crying at the kitchen sink in front of his ten-year-old son is much more healthy than Daddy's sneaking out into the garage to cry behind closed doors. Secret-keeping and denial are common modes of operation in some families. However, this mode of operation does not model healthy grieving to children. When the thoughts and feelings of other family members are kept inside and difficult topics are never discussed, this can be confusing to children who have been told, "You can come to me about anything honey. There's nothing we can't talk about."

Sometimes the death of a loved one is so painful and overwhelming, initially, that the adults in the family are not able to "be there" for their children emotionally. When grief is fresh and family members are feeling raw and numb, sometimes the presence of caring adults from the church or neighborhood can be very helpful to grieving children. Taking the child out for an ice cream sundae or inviting him to hit baseballs at the batting cage might be a way to let him know that you, as a caring adult, are concerned about him during this hard time in his life. Taking time on a Saturday morning to come over to repair a tree house or to go on a walk with a grieving girl and her family dog might help her feel less alone in her grief.

In some cultures, it is traditional to view the entire community as responsible for raising children. While Americans traditionally do not hold to the value of "It takes a whole community to raise children," I am a proponent of uplifting this model when death and other losses affect children in our communities and congregations. The death of a relative or loved one can be a lonely and sad experience for both children and adults. As Christians, Jesus Christ exhorts us to extend his grace and his healing hand to those who are hurting and broken.

In his letter to the Christians in Rome, Paul writes about believers being part of the "body of Christ." As members of the "body of Christ," each member of the body has something special or unique to offer to the whole. In Romans 12, Paul writes about the variety of gifts that God has given to believers to be used to build up the Christian community. One of those seven gifts is the gift of being compassionate and of extending mercy towards others (v. 8). Following his recitations of what he perceives to be the gifts that members of the body of Christ are given by God, Paul follows these verses by issuing exhortation to believers. Sharing the pain and the hardships of fellow believers is included in Paul's exhortation. "Rejoice with those who rejoice, and weep with those who weep" (v. 15).

In 1972, Bill Withers' hit song, "Lean On Me," was released. This song has become a familial sing-along at children's grief camps as camp leaders encourage grieving children to find someone to walk with them during their grief journeys. The point of the song is to encourage grievers to allow others to look to others for support and strength when encountering painful times in their lives.[1]

When grieving children have the support of caring adults in their lives who are not emotionally involved in the loss that is being grieved, children are given the opportunity to benefit from the compassion and the strength of others. While friends and congregational members have little control of stopping bad things from happening to children, we are capable of providing them with love and support during their time of grief and loss. Even though some of these factors listed in this chapter are outside our control, I believe that with God's help we can assist our younger sisters and brothers in Christ in expressing their grief following the death of a loved one.

---

1. Complete lyrics to "Lean On Me," written by Bill Withers, can be found at http://www.weddingvendors.com/music/lyrics/b/bill-withers.

Defining Grief And Mourning

"Stop giving me grief. You like to see me squirm, don't you?" Adults sometimes like to tease or harass others by "causing them grief." When the implication is that one person is jokingly "causing grief" to another person, this type of grief is quite different from talking about grief as the pain or the suffering that results when someone loved has died or when something treasured has been taken away from a person.

One afternoon on the golf course, I repeatedly hit a number of balls into the sand traps and out of bounds. My golfing partner started to hassle me about my poor performance. She said, "And remind me now, how long have you been playing this game? Why do you pay money to torture yourself like this? When I see you continually losing your temper after each bad shot, I know I am going to beat you." Then she began to laugh. She knew that not only was my game getting worse by the moment, but her comments were intended to "rattle my chain." While she did not intend to make me angry by her words, her goal was to make fun of me and get a laugh from the other two ladies who were listening in on our conversation.

In this situation, my friend was trying to "cause me grief." Her intentions were not to anger me so much that I would quit playing golf; rather, she wanted to hassle me a little in a joking fashion. Having this type of grief inflicted upon me was nothing like the grief I felt when my best friend died in a tornado at the age of 25. Nor was this grief anything like the sadness and depression I felt when my father died 87 days after being diagnosed with lung cancer.

Defining how the word grief is used in the context of death and other types of loss seems necessary and appropriate. Grief is how a person responds to loss. The word "grief" implies that when someone we have loved has died or when something valued has been taken away or removed, this causes some type of reaction. Grief, therefore, is an internal experience or a reaction to a loss. Children grieve when someone they loved has died. Likewise, many children grieve when other losses occur, such as when their parents divorce, their home is destroyed by a fire, or if their favorite plush animal from infancy is stolen or destroyed. While no two children will respond to a loss in the exact same manner, every child will respond in some way to the absence of the lost person or thing.

Often people use the word "mourning" synonymously with the word "grief." While the two words are closely linked to loss, there is a difference between the words "grief" and "mourning." While grief relates to the internal experience of a person who is responding to the loss, mourning is the public expression of that person's grief. While grief is how a person internalizes his feelings of loss, mourning is more the process that occurs after the loss. Another way to define "mourning" is to describe it as the public or cultural display of one's grief through one's behaviors. Dr. Alan Wolfelt, the director of the Center for Life and Loss Transition in Fort Collins, Colorado, simply defines mourning as "grief gone public."

Often people assume that children are doing "fine" following a loss because they may not witness firsthand a child publicly displaying any emotions of sadness or depression. While a child might return to school a week after a sibling's death and appear to be coping well, the child's public behavior may not be consistent with his internal feelings about the death of his baby sister. Like adults, some children hide their innermost feelings from others. Henceforth, to the public, a grieving child may appear to be doing okay when internally he or she may be feeling overwhelmed, severely depressed, or lonely.

Sometimes when children are older or if they are large for their age, adults might think of them as behaving more adultlike than childlike. While teenagers are cognitively capable of having more adultlike thoughts and attitudes, adults need to remember that teenagers are still children. In one of the congregations where I served, a distant relative told the fifteen-year-old son that as a result of his father's death, he was now "the man of the house." Inflicting adultlike roles onto children is not fair to children, nor will it help them embrace their feelings of grief.

Children grieve like children and not like adults. Even though well-intentioned adults can impose their expectations and hopes onto a grieving child, it is unfair and not realistic to expect a child to behave in any way other than in an age-appropriate manner. While a seventeen-year-old boy might weigh 200 pounds and sport a full beard, internally he is still a child and should be given permission to express his grief in a way that feels appropriate and healthy for him.

Children will grieve the death of a loved one according to their developmental level. How seventeen-year-old Hillary grieves for her mother will be different from how her ten-year-old brother, Jim, grieves for Mom. Smaller children obviously have less experience with loss and often are not sure what to do with all their feelings and thoughts. Older children might have more experience with loss and more cognitive abilities. Sometimes age and maturity can lead older children to question the fairness and the meaning of life.

Because no two human beings are alike, no two people will grieve alike. When death impacts the life of children, adults often feel helpless and inadequate. Reading books like this can help caring adults to better understand how children understand death and may grieve the loss of someone to death. No one book is intended to provide the "quick fix." On the other hand, reading books, talking to others who have companioned children through their grief journeys, and observing how children are acting and behaving can be helpful in assisting you to walk with grieving children.

While many adults find it helpful to talk about their grief and allow others to be part of their mourning process, children are less apt to verbalize their innermost feelings. Grief counselors who work with children do not have their offices set up like counselors do who work primarily with adults. In an office where children are the primary clients, one will find plush toys, dolls, puppets, art supplies, whiteboards, and so on. Most children are better at playing out their grief than verbalizing it. Caring adults who are willing to play with children and who will allow children to control what is played, will get a better understanding of how a child is grieving, than will an adult who says to a child, "Tell me how you are feeling today."

Play is as natural to a child as stretching is to an animal after a lengthy sleep. Playing is how children naturally express themselves. While it is not instinctual from birth for children to talk, it is instinctual for children to play. Small children have short attention spans and will, therefore, jump from one thing to another quite frequently. Even though caring adults might find this frustrating, this is how small children play. Supporting and enabling children in expressing their grief is not easy work for many adults. Sometimes, being with children forces adults to move beyond their comfort zone. However, if the goal is to help children to embrace their grief over the death of a loved one, caring adults need to remember that spending time with grieving children is about meeting the needs of children, not meeting their own needs.

Children grieve in spurts. Unlike adults who might want to talk about their feelings for thirty minutes or an hour at a time with a relative or friends, children often can only absorb pain and discomfort for short periods of time. One minute, eight-year-old Miranda may be playing with her Barbie™ dolls where Barbie™ is telling Ken™ that she is too sad to jump into the doll swimming pool with him. Five minutes later, Miranda may say that it is time now to go outside and play kickball. Expressing her sadness for five minutes through Barbie's™ interaction with Ken™ may be all that Miranda can handle at the moment. She needs time to run and let her mind think of something more fun and more positive.

When the loss that is being grieved is the death of a relative or close friend, caring adults need to be aware of secondary losses that may have occurred. A secondary loss is a physical or a psychosocial loss that coincides with, or develops as, a consequence of the initial loss. Examples of physical loss might include moving out of one's home, having one's treasured possessions taken away or removed, experiencing one's best friend moving to another school, or seeing one's church destroyed by a fire. Psychosocial losses might include the divorce of one's parents, getting fired from one's job, losing one's dream, or one's loss of trust in the world due to bad things happening in the community or to the person's immediate family. While a physical loss is the loss of something tangible or the loss of someone, a psychosocial loss is the loss of something intangible, psychosocial in nature.

When fourteen-year-old Curt's older brother died by suicide, Curt's whole world was turned upside down. One year after his brother's death, Curt's parents separated and filed for divorce. Because their marriage was in deep distress prior to the suicide, the death of the couple's oldest son put an additional strain on the marriage that neither person was willing to address. When the separation took place, Curt's parents forced their youngest son to choose where he wanted to live. When Curt was forced to admit that his mother's drinking was hard for him to handle, Curt's dad used that information in the courtroom to obtain custody of his son.

Two years after Curt's brother's suicide, Curt was experiencing many secondary losses resulting from the death. His brother was no longer there to talk with and to be his confidant. Previously they were best of friends. Following his parents' divorce, Curt's relationship with his mother deteriorated. No longer did his mother and he play tennis together or go hiking. The loss of his sporting companion as well as the loss of his mother as a sounding board for his poetry and creative writing was difficult for Curt. In addition to these secondary losses, other secondary losses following the death included having to move out of their big home in the suburbs into a small apartment with his father and the loss of his girlfriend who wanted nothing to do with someone whose brother had committed suicide.

When secondary losses are numerous, this complicates further the grieving process for children. Death is difficult enough for children; however, when secondary losses are added into the picture this can complicate and extend the grieving process. Another important term to be familiar with is that of multiple losses. Sometimes secondary and multiple losses go hand in hand, other times they do not. While the divorce of Curt's parents and his having to move out of his suburban house were secondary losses that resulted following his brother's suicide, multiple losses are sometimes not directly related.

Multiple losses for children might include the death of a close relative, which is followed in close proximity by the death of a schoolteacher, and then the accidental death of the family's dog. When children experience a number of deaths or losses in a short period of time, family members and caring adults need to continue to keep the communication lines open. Grieving children need to know that there are people around who are willing to talk or play with them.

When teenagers experience multiple losses, family members need to give the children permission to spend time with peers. During the age of adolescence, peer support is where most teenagers will find support. Sometimes friends or other caring adults have the greatest opportunity to provide grieving teenagers a safe place of consolation. Instead of taking this as a personal rejection, family members are advised to keep the best interest of children in mind. In the case of multiple losses, sometimes children do not want to burden their parents, especially if the children perceive that their parents are grieving the same losses that they are grieving. When this is the case, other friends or adults are truly the best caregivers and supporters, provided that these caring adults are not emotionally connected to the losses.

Another important factor to be aware of when encountering grieving individuals is what is called "regrieving." Six-year-old Constanza lost her mother after a short bout with breast cancer. Initially, Constanza experienced a great deal of separation pain and sadness. As the first day of school approached in the fall, Constanza was not only sad that her mother was absent from sharing this experience with her, but Constanza felt a great deal of anger when she heard two classmates complaining about their mothers during lunch on the first day of school. Constanza was angry that her mother had died. She was also angry that it was her grandmother who was given custody over her and her eight-year-old brother. Constanza resented being around other children who were rude or unappreciative of their mothers.

In time, Constanza was able to express her feelings of sadness and anger. A grief counselor and her family's pastor helped Constanza to embrace many of her feelings and to talk about her fears. As the years went on, Constanza repeatedly regrieved her mother's death. When Constanza went on her first date at fifteen, she grieved about not having a mother around for advice. Attending her first prom was also very difficult for her. While most of her girlfriends had mothers who went dress shopping with them or who accompanied their daughters for pedicures, Constanza felt very lonely.

While her father had abandoned the family when Constanza was quite young, not having either parent at her high school graduation sent the adolescent into a deep depression. Her maternal aunt and a special next-door neighbor were able to be companions to Constanza during that difficult period of her life. Without her aunt and her neighbor, Constanza wrote in her journal that she might have given suicide more than a fleeting thought. No one had prepared her for the process of regrieving in the years that had followed her mother's death. Constanza was a fortunate young woman to be able to find other caring adults in her life to assist her during her grief process.

Swiss-American psychiatrist, Dr. Elisabeth Kübler-Ross, wrote about the stages that some people experience when they know that they are dying. In her book, *On Death and Dying*, which was published in 1969, Kübler-Ross elaborates about five stages that many terminally ill people experience. These stages are as follows: denial, anger, bargaining, depression, and acceptance. Over the years Kübler-Ross' stages have come to be accepted as stages of grieving, as well. While these five stages often are applicable to grievers, in many instances, grieving individuals experience many other feelings in addition to denial, anger, bargaining, depression, and acceptance. In a later chapter, I will go into greater detail about some of the grief reactions that children might experience after a loved one has died.

Throughout this book, I refer to grief and mourning as a process that people experience when someone loved has died or when something treasured has been taken or removed from them. While no time line can be set as to how long grieving or mourning lasts, experts have come to believe that there are phases or tasks that grievers need to complete or work through before their mourning can be successfully completed.

Dr. J. William Worden, clinical psychologist and codirector the Harvard Child Bereavement Study, developed the "Four Tasks of Mourning" that grief counselors today generally recognize as being very helpful in working with grieving individuals. According to Worden's model, experiencing grief takes work and effort. It is not a passive process, but an active one. In order for a person to move through their grief in a healthy manner, the grieving individual needs to be an active participant in their own healing. When the grieving individual is a child, family members and caring adults will need to accompany the child in the mourning process.

The first task of mourning is "accepting the reality of the loss." Since small children are not able to understand the permanence of death, this task will usually not be completed by children under the age of five. However, as children develop their cognitive abilities, they are better able to comprehend the finality of death. In order to complete this first task of mourning, grieving individuals need to accept the fact that their loved one is dead and will not return. A reunion with that person is no longer possible here on earth. While we know that sometimes grievers frantically search for their loved one hoping to find him or her still alive, in order to do the work of mourning, the griever must accept the fact that their loved one is gone.

Coming to terms with the death of someone loved, especially in the case of sudden death, is very difficult for most people. For adults, the emotional acceptance of a loved one's death is generally harder than the intellectual acceptance. In the case of children, young children do not have the cognitive abilities of older children or adults; therefore, some children have a hard time both cognitively and emotionally. What they need is patience and time. When death touches the lives of children, unconditional love and acceptance are of utmost importance.

Allowing children to attend the visitation time and the funeral can often be helpful in assisting them to move toward acceptance. The more children are around others who are willing to talk about the death and who are willing to embrace their feelings, the better.

When children are included in things "that matter the most," this not only helps them to feel an important part of the family, but it also gives them permission to embrace what has happened. The more children are given permission to participate in the funeral, to receive support from their community, and to express their feelings, the more likely they will be to move toward accepting the reality of the loss.

"Working through to the pain of grief" is the second task of mourning. Experience has shown that some people are better at admitting their pain and acknowledging their innermost feelings than are others. Some people think that if they bury their feelings and deny their pain, it will go away in time. On the other hand, most of us know that there are other people who are willing to admit their vulnerability and who are more open to acknowledge and to embrace their pain.

Dr. Worden states that it is necessary to acknowledge and to work through the pain, or it will manifest itself through physical symptoms or some form of behavioral reaction. When children have a stomachache for an extended period of time or start having migraines following the death of someone loved, this may be an indication that there is repressed grief. A five-year-old child may no longer be able to control his bowels or have the strength to lift a small dog food bag because he is grieving the death of his mommy but does not know what to do about it since his father forbids him from talking about it. Other children who are in emotional pain over the death of someone loved might become school bullies or suddenly become "the bad children" in Sunday school.

Children need to find ways to embrace their grief and express their feelings. Like adults, simply keeping children busy or discouraging them from expressing their grief are not healthy techniques. Pain over the death of someone loved needs to be experienced and worked through. While a sore tooth might go away on its own, grief does not operate like that. Like a sore on a person's body, the pus and the infected fluids need to get out. If the pain is buried or unattended to, it will resurface in the future. As family members or caring adults, you may need to help grieving children find ways to work through their pain and express it. While this is sometimes difficult, it is a very important part of the mourning process.

The third task of mourning is "to adjust to an environment in which the deceased is missing." When children lose a parent to death, children often do not know how their lives will continue. Children may ask the following questions upon the death of a parent: "Who am I now that Daddy is dead? Who will take care of my brother and me? Who is going to feed us every day and drive me to school?"

When people die, roles in families change and shift. Given the absence of a family member, others will have to do things that the loved one once completed. With Mom's death, someone will now have to drive Patty to school. Someone will have to pack her lunch, as well. This new person who packs Patty's lunch will no doubt do it differently than Mom did. Patty will have to adjust to many changes in her home and in her everyday life. Roles change in a family when death takes place. Sometimes people have to learn new skills or be willing to take on new jobs or responsibilities. This is called "role reorganization."

Children are often capable of accepting new jobs or roles if they are age-appropriate and not overburdening. Since she is school-aged, Patty is capable of feeding her dog before going to school. She may also be capable of getting the mail out of the mailbox and placing it on her father's desk as she walks up the driveway after school. While adults often take on the most jobs and new roles upon the death of loved ones, children are also capable of adjusting to these changes given time, patience, and understanding.

While things may never go back to the way they were prior to the death, children are capable of grasping the notion that death truly does change things. Following the death of someone loved, life will return to normalcy one day. However, this normalcy will be "a new normal." Things do change. With children it is important to recognize that adjusting to changes are not always easy nor welcome. Again, grieving children need to be given love, patience, and understanding.

"Emotionally relocating the deceased and moving on with life" is the fourth task according to Dr. Worden's model. During this final task, the grieving person is able to move forward with their lives and start forming new relationships. Instead of holding on to the past, a person is now able to move forward. It is important that people understand what is being said here is not that grievers will *ever forget* the person who died, but our loved ones will always be remembered and valued. On the other hand, in this fourth task, the griever is no longer preoccupied with thinking about the deceased all the time and constantly feeling pain.

Essentially, the grieving individual has found a new place for this person emotionally. The griever is not giving up nor ending his relationship with the loved one; rather, he is finding a new and appropriate place for the dead person in his emotional life. In this final task, there is an emotional letting go. It is also during this task that the grieving person is now able to initiate new relationships. These new relationships are not intended to replace the loved one; rather, it is a sign that the griever realizes that life must be lived forward.

When fourteen-year-old Sam's girlfriend was killed in a canoeing accident, Sam hurt all over for months. He vowed to never let another person into his heart like he had let Tammy. They had known each other since first grade. Because their parents were such good friends, the families vacationed together and also attended the same church. At the meal following the funeral, Sam told his friends who were sitting at the table that he would never allow another girl into his life again. He vowed to not even have a girl for a best friend. That was just too risky for another painful ending.

About a year after Tammy's death, a new girl transferred to Sam's school. Nellie met Sam on his first day in her new school. After getting lost in the hallway between third and fourth periods, Sam offered to show her where the chemistry lab was located. A week later, Sam invited Nellie to his church for the congregation's potluck dinner and youth dance. Even though he had no intentions of dating Nellie, in time they became close friends. Sam's ability to make a new friend who happened to be female indicated that he was ready to emotionally move on with his life. In time, Sam realized that he had to look to the future. He could not stay stuck in the past. While never forgetting Tammy, Sam got married at the age of

25 and had two daughters. On the wall in his den hangs a picture of Tammy and Sam roasting marshmallows during one of their families' camping trips.

Some people have described the death of a loved one as one of those life experiences where a hole has been placed in their hearts. When people we love die, some of us have acknowledged that we feel like a tremendous hole has damaged our hearts. We feel empty. We feel broken and incomplete. However, in time, most grieving individuals have come to discover that the hole has gotten smaller. The hole never completely goes away because we are changed by our loss. There will always be a small hole. We do not "get over" grief like we "get over" the flu. Death does change us. Healthy grievers are those people who decide to embrace their grief and move toward it. Instead of burying the pain and repressing it, experience shows that in time, grievers can actually grow and learn from their loss and from their pain.

When grieving individuals are able to reinvest their emotions back into living and look toward the future, these individuals are most likely near the completion of their mourning work. Certainly the loved ones will not be forgotten. Life is now different. Death changes everything, including us!

How Children Understand Death

In this chapter, a developmental understanding of death will be presented. While the age-level understanding of children will be divided into five different developmental stages, it is important to understand that this is a guide, not a rigid and unbending stage theory. Because of differences in maturity, intellect, life experiences, the influence of one's family, and other factors that were touched upon in chapter 3, some children might actually fit better in the earlier or the later stage than some of their same-aged peers.

This chapter is intended to serve as a guide to explain how children may understand death. Your child may deviate from the model that is being proposed here. Do not take that to mean that your child is abnormal. It is important to remember that each child is unique. No two children are alike!

For the purposes of this book, I have separated the developmental stages of children into five parts. Stage one includes children in infancy and toddlerhood. The next stage begins around age three and incorporates preschool children up to five years old. Stage three is made up of children who are early school age. In this developmental level, we find children aged five through nine. In the fourth stage, children aged nine through twelve are at the early adolescence level. The final developmental stage contains adolescents who are thirteen and older.

Stage One — Infancy And Toddlerhood

From the instant that newborn babies emerge from their mother's womb, they are completely dependent upon others for survival. As soon as parents take their newborns home from the hospital, young children depend heavily upon their parents or caretakers. Infants and toddlers generally have one person in their lives that functions as their "attachment figure." While many different people can provide love and care for small children, during this developmental stage, infants and toddlers form a strong attachment bond to one person. When separated from this person, small children often protest by crying or screaming uncontrollably.

Anyone who has ever watched an anxious father try to comfort a screaming one-year-old, soon realizes that when Mommy leaves the child in the grocery story and disappears from the child's eyesight, the father will have his hands full for quite a while. "Separation anxiety" is a very real phenomenon. Infants and toddlers can also be fearful of being abandoned by other caring people in their lives, besides their mothers. Fathers, babysitters, an older sibling, or a very loving and attentive relative can serve as attachment figures.

Infants and toddlers are not capable of understanding the permanence of death. They may cry or scream for a very long time. Children of this age are not able to comprehend that death means that their loved one will not return. Children in this developmental stage are not capable of understanding the difference between their mother going out of town for a three-day business trip and the reality of their father being killed in a car crash on the way home from work. Being abandoned or being separated from a loved one can cause great unrest and distress in young children.

However, while infants and toddlers are not able to comprehend the permanence of death, we should not interpret that to mean that they are incapable of feeling sadness or loneliness when a loved one dies. It is possible that at this age, young children are able to respond emotionally to the feelings of loss or separation from a loved one, even though they will not comprehend what has actually occurred is death.

Young children, much like some pets, are quite sensitive to the emotions of others around them. When a loved one dies and family members express their sadness, infants and children can often pick up on this. Often, young children will cry when others around them are sobbing. When there is sadness or anxiety in their homes, some children will experience changes in their eating, sleeping, and crying patterns. An eleven-month-old baby, who normally could sleep all night, may begin to wake up repeatedly in the night upon the death of his grandmother. A two-year-old may hardly eat anything for two weeks after his brother and dog were killed.

While unable to cognitively understand that death means they will never see their loved one again, infants and toddlers are often very capable of emotionally reacting to the death of someone loved. If the person the young child was most attached to dies, caring adults and family members should be prepared for the infant or toddler to react behaviorally to the absence of this loved one. To not experience some type of emotional reaction would be more uncommon than common, except in cases when young children are intentionally sheltered from the grief of those around them.

Some pets, dogs in particular, are very sensitive to emotions like depression and crying. Infants and toddlers are likewise more sensitive and more attuned to the emotionality of others than some folks might like to admit. While you might think that your new-born is oblivious to the fact that his grandfather died, do not be surprised when baby Jonathan's cooing shifts to crying when Mom receives the news over the telephone. As Mom begins crying, little Jonathan might begin to cry, also.

Infants and toddlers do not understand death but are capable of reacting to the emotions of others. While they do not understand the permanence of death, infants and toddlers can react to death through changes in their behavior. Because of their dependence and attachment issues, children who are under the age of three often fear being abandoned, especially from loved ones with whom they spend a large amount of time.

Stage Two — Preschool (3-5 years old)

By the time children reach the age of three, they are completely egocentric. During the preschool years, children are said to be at the "age of curiosity"; at the same time, they view everything through the lens of their own experience. While young children at this level of development will ask many questions and will be very curious, they will not be able to understand that which they have not personally experienced. A difficult concept for young children to comprehend at this age is that people think and feel differently than they do. When asking questions, if preschoolers are ignored or do not get answers, they will use their imaginations to come up with possible explanations.

Preschool children are prone to operate by what is called "magical thinking." This means that children who are three to five years old think that their wishes can really come true. For many of them, life is like a fairy tale, and their minds are full of fantasies. If you wish for something, then it can come true. However, this kind of magical thinking can also have negative effects on children.

If a child became angry and wished that someone was dead, and for some reason that person actually died, then the child might feel it was that wish that caused the death. A colleague once told me that a four-year-old in his church membership felt responsible for her cousin's death. Apparently, the four-year-old was jealous of her cousin, and several times wished the cousin was dead. After her cousin was killed by a drunk driver, the four-year-old blamed herself for the death.

During this stage of development, young children are beginning to master language. As they continue to acquire better vocabularies, they will simultaneously be able to use their minds in ways that they were unable to as infants or toddlers. With this increasing ability to speak and think, preschoolers will now begin to muse more frequently about death.

While these children are no longer completely dependent upon their parents as they were as infants, preschoolers have gained some autonomy and are beginning to take some initiative on their own. Even though this is the case, the thought of being abandoned or separated from their parent or caretaker is likely to stir up some anxiety and possibly fear.

Preschool-age children often perceive death to be something temporary, like sleeping or taking a trip. One minute, a person is here, and the next minute, he or she has departed. It can be compared to when a parent or loved one goes to work, and is later expected to return home. In other words, preschoolers cannot comprehend the fact that death means that a loved one will never come back. They think death is like being asleep. A person who is asleep will later wake up.

Preschoolers think that even in the coffin, their loved one continues to live, but somewhat differently than before. Many children aged three to five think that a dead person who has been placed in a coffin still breathes, eats, and is aware of what is going on in the outside world.

Children of that age often view death as gradual and temporary. Because they do not understand death, they use their imaginations to explain what they think happens at death. For example, preschoolers may view death in different stages or as a gradual process such as noting the difference in time between when a body has been placed in the casket and several days later after the casket has been buried and dirt has been placed all around it. While preschoolers may seem to understand that death means a separation from them, in the next breath they might explain to you that their loved one's death is reversible because they are not able to accept the finality of death.

Because of their limited life experiences, children in this age group tend to think of death as that which is accidental. They cannot comprehend the notion that death is inevitable because in their minds a person only dies under certain conditions. According to preschoolers, these conditions may or may not happen. Most definitely they believe they will not die because they are not old or very sick, and because they cannot imagine that a car accident or a murder could ever happen to them.

To summarize this developmental stage, preschoolers often do not understand death to be final. Children three to five years old do not think that death is inevitable. It will certainly not happen to them! While most adults know that death is a normal part of life, ask a preschooler and he or she will be quick to inform you that death is not a normal part of life. It happens to others, but not to them and to those they love the most.

Stage Three — Early School Age (5-9 years old)

About the time young children begin school, they have begun to ask questions about the world and how things around them operate. At this stage of development, children are like little scientists who are seeking to obtain answers to life's little mysteries. While in preschool, they could not grasp the relationship between causes and effects, now children are beginning to label objects and are starting to understand that some events occur in response to specific causes. For example, six-year-old Jamal now understands that if his mother does not remind him to regularly feed his fish and keep the fish tank clean, he might find several of his beloved fish floating on top of the water.

As early school-age children are beginning to explore the workings of the world, they are now starting to ask biological questions. Children want to know about bones and blood at this stage of their development. The whereabouts of a pet's body after it has been buried is a common question at this age. In their play, reenacting a pet's death or a fatal heart attack like they had observed on television the night before would not be a strange occurrence. While adults might find this playacting offensive, this would be a natural reaction for this age group.

At this age, children have gradually accepted the notion that death is final and inevitable. Despite their earlier thoughts that all things that moved were living, now they are beginning to recognize that all people, animals, and plant life are living entities. With this realization, they have come to accept the fact that those things which live, must also die. Herein, school-age children are now beginning to comprehend that death is something which is irreversible.

While they may be able to accept the fact that some people do die, at the same time many children in this age group are not able to accept death in their own lives. While death is on their minds at this age, early school-age children are more likely to keep their feelings to themselves, whereas preschoolers are more apt to share them with parents. With all of these thoughts and unexpressed feelings tossing around in their heads, it is understandable why children at this level of development neither deny nor are truly able to accept death in their own lives, or in the lives of those most close to them. For children of this age, death is generally perceived to result from accidents or as a result of old age or a lengthy illness.

Many early school-age children personify death. This means that they think of death as a person or some type of evil being that comes and takes people away. When asked to draw what death is like, children in this age group often draw pictures of skeletons, ghosts, witches, monsters, or boogeymen. Generally this perception seems to be linked to the notion that an evil being comes in the dark to perform the violent act of taking another person's life. While some people might be kidnapped or killed by this boogeyman or monster, other people might be lucky enough or clever enough to be spared. Some children believe that if they are clever enough or good enough in behavior, they might be able to avoid the boogeyman or the ghost of death.

While five- to nine-year-old children want to know all the gory details about how the family on the nightly news actually died, they are thoroughly frightened when they think about the possibility of some ghostly creature coming after them in the middle of the night. At this age, death anxiety is rampant in children. As individuals who are becoming more competent in their ability to perform and understand things, they continue to be afraid of being abandoned by their parents, and now also worry about the fear of bodily injury or the possibility that God might punish them for their bad behaviors.

Children in this age bracket are capable of understanding that death is final. While they realize that all things die, on the other hand, they cannot accept that death might happen to them. Early school-age children are like scientists who ask lots of biological questions. They are very interested in blood, gore, and guts. However, because many children in this developmental stage personify death, death anxiety is often prevalent.

Stage Four — Early Adolescence (9-12 years old)

Around the age of nine or ten, children are beginning to have more adult thoughts and understandings. While they are starting to develop a more mature understanding of life and death, they still ask childlike questions and also retain many childish fears and anxieties.

As children grow and develop mentally and intellectually, they will continue to act like inquisitive scientists at this age. Despite the fact that adults are often uncomfortable with their questions, children at this developmental stage resume their interest in what happens to a dead person's body. Early adolescents want to know what will happen after a casket has been buried, and the body is left permanently underground.

Early adolescent children are very concerned about funeral practices and burial rituals, and they need someone to help them understand the whereabouts of their loved one. By gaining data and insight regarding what happens at death, children of this age will gain control over some of their fears and anxieties. If no one is there to provide them with answers or hope, then they may briefly return to magical thinking in order to cope with their thoughts or feelings.

While these children are fairly capable of coming up with some of their own conclusions and opinions by now, it is normal for children of this age to begin to accept their family's spiritual beliefs about life and death. It is during this age of development that death is beginning to become more spiritual and abstract.

At this stage of development, children are able to understand that upon death, a person is no longer alive, and his or her body no longer functions as it did while living. Dead people no longer breathe, eat, go to the bathroom, or experience pain. When eleven-year-old Tomas attends the visitation at the local funeral home upon the death of his beloved aunt, he knows that when he touches his aunt's body, it will feel stiff and be free of pain. Tomas knows that what he is touching is merely a physical shell, which is no longer alive.

From age nine and beyond, children are able to understand that death is inevitable and universal. Children are now able to acknowledge that everyone, including themselves, will die. And while this might still evoke fear and uncertainty for children, many of these same children will now have some awareness of an after-life following physical death.

During this stage of development, early adolescents are becoming more aware of the emotional aspects of death, as well. They are also more cognizant of the feelings of others in response to the loss, and are therefore capable of being included in some of the adult conversations about the death and the pain, which may have accompanied it. If they are aware of what has transpired with a loved one's death, early adolescents are now able to empathize and may want to provide emotional support to those they see who are hurting.

Toward the end of this stage, children are starting to move away from only concrete thoughts and are beginning to think more abstractly. They are starting to realize that death is not some outside or exterior force that comes after you; rather, death is a normal part of life. Previously children were of the opinion that they could avoid death if they were clever or lucky, now they understand that death happens to both the young and the old. Death is no longer personified, but it has natural causes. A person may die as a result of a natural disaster, a car accident, a school shooting, a disease, or simply because one's body was too weak to continue functioning.

Despite the fact that most children from nine to twelve years old are able to think like adults in some ways, one must remember that they are still children in other aspects of their development. Even though they know that many people who die are much older than they, early adolescents still worry about their own mortality. Children at this age worry about pain and the possibility of suffering when they think of their own death or the death of someone they love. Because of their increased exposure to the media, children today are much more aware of the possibility of terrorism, nuclear war, and large-scale destruction. This can also be a cause of anxiety for children.

To summarize this developmental stage, early adolescents understand fully that dead is dead. A person who has died no longer breathes, eats, or experiences pain. Death is final and universal. Children in this age group comprehend that death can have natural or accidental causes. Along with these abilities to comprehend death comes an awareness of spirituality and a sensitivity to the emotional reactions of others.

Stage Five — Adolescence (13-18 years old)

Anyone who has spent much time around adolescents knows that these growing and maturing individuals are much different than are any other children. One might say that adolescents are "a new breed of cat." During the teenage years, adolescents are struggling to determine their identities and are often engrossed in themselves. In many ways, teenagers are very egocentric in their cognitions and behaviors, thinking that their parents and other adults around them know very little in comparison to them.

Adolescence is a very difficult time for many children. While on the outside, adolescents work to put on a good front, on the inside many teenagers are struggling with figuring out who they want to become and what they want to do with their futures. Developing their identities and their place in life is where most teenagers are developmentally at this time. It is also at this developmental stage that children who are thirteen and beyond are confronted with keeping promises, making commitments, and setting goals for the future. Learning some adult responsibilities and being faithful to friendships and relationships are new challenges for adolescents.

Despite the fact that early adolescents only begin to think like adults, teenagers have actually become more like adults in most of their thinking. Because adolescents are searching for meaning and purpose in their lives, this causes them to think more deeply about things than ever before. Teenagers will now philosophize and consider every possible way situations might be addressed or approached before taking a firm position on any important topic. Even though at times they might not think things through completely, they are much more likely to speculate and hypothesize before making significant decisions and choices.

With the increased hormones and sexual drive, adolescents now have to determine how to handle all these new feelings and possibilities. Besides making sexual decisions and developing a sense of self, teenagers are also coming to the realization that the world now treats them more like adults. Despite the fact that they still lack the life experience of most adults, adolescents are capable of having deep and intellectual conversations with adults and being equal participants in those dialogues.

With this increased cognitive ability, adolescents are now capable of fully understanding death like adults. Gone forever is the thinking that death is some ghost or boogeyman that is out to get them. Now children fully understand that death is as natural a part of life as birth is. As teenagers are developing their new identities and are forced to make choices regarding their goals for the future, they must now figure out how death fits into their understanding of the world.

Teenagers are fully aware that death is inevitable and irreversible. They may have known people who lived healthy lifestyles by eating well and exercising but they also know that this is no guarantee for a long and prosperous life. Life is fragile, and no one knows when the phone will ring and someone will be on the other end to be the bearer of tragic news. Despite knowing other children or teenagers who may have died in accidents, from suicide, or from a disease, most teenagers tend to think of death as that which remains distant from them. This is because most adolescents think of themselves as being invincible.

Many children who are between the ages of thirteen and eighteen view death as the enemy. In other words, death has the power to erase all of their hopes and dreams for the future. Since teenagers are engrossed in their looks and their bodies, their friendships, and their career possibilities at this age, the notion of dying is something they would like to forget or repress.

Even though most adolescents would like to forget about death so that they can focus on themselves and their futures, teenagers actually spend a great deal of time thinking about death. With their intellectual and philosophical abilities, teenagers often look to find a psychological or spiritual meaning for death as part of their greater search to understand life. During this stage of maturation, adolescents will most likely assume their parents' religious or spiritual beliefs, but will certainly ponder them before taking full ownership of these beliefs.

In their younger years, children would often look to their parents for support and for further explanation about subjects that concerned them. Teenagers, however, will often turn to their peers or other adults when they want to talk about serious topics like death or the afterlife. In many cases, a parent will be the last person a teenager will feel comfortable talking to about such subjects.

When facilitating a grief group at a local high school, one of the students was wrestling with what had occurred after the death of her brother. Because she was not comfortable talking to her parents about her brother's death or many other serious topics for that matter, she chose to raise the question of the afterlife with her peers and the two adult grief group facilitators. I came to believe that this student did not really want someone else to tell her what to believe, rather she merely needed a safe place to raise a question that was on her mind.

Many teenagers do not want to show vulnerability and weakness to their friends or to the adults around them. Because of their feelings of invincibility, children who are in their latter teenage years will sometimes drive the car too fast or drink too much alcohol in order to prove to themselves how powerful they are. For some adolescents, this may be the only way they know how to cope with their fears about death.

If caring adults want to know how much death and death-related themes and thoughts are on the mind of adolescents, simply listen to the music or take notice of the movies and television programs that they are listening to and watching. In their free time, many adolescents listen to music or watch television shows and movies that are full of themes focusing around dying, suicide, violence, war, drugs, and so on.

With these influences in their lives, combined with society's view of them as adultlike in their thinking, life for many adolescents is difficult. At times, some teenagers may wish to return to an earlier stage of childhood where life appeared to be simpler. On the other hand, most adolescents do want to be grown up and become their own person. This means that they will have to continue to ponder how death and the end of a person's physical life fits into their understanding of the world. Moving out of childhood into adulthood "is not always what it is cracked up to be."

To summarize this developmental stage, adolescents have come to accept that death is a natural part of life and that death is inevitable and irreversible. Simultaneously, they see it as a threat to end all their hopes and dreams; many adolescents think of death as their enemy. Much of what entertains teenagers today indicates that they are highly exposed to death themes. It is in their thoughts more often than many adults realize. And with the increased cognitive ability and maturity of children who are thirteen to eighteen years old, adolescents often give serious consideration to their parents' religious or spiritual beliefs and often come to own them personally.

By understanding how children understand death and how they think given their age group, caring adults are more able to help grieving children embrace their grief upon the death of a loved one. Realizing that this information on developmental stages is merely a guide, adults need to recognize that no two children will grieve alike. Caring adults also need to acknowledge that some children may grieve in the stages behind or ahead of same-aged children, depending on individual circumstances.

Types Of Grief Reactions

As the children sat on the floor on beanbag chairs and talked about the death of their loved one, it was apparent that each child's grief was unique. While all the children had experienced the death of a loved one, how each child responded to the loss was different from that of the child sitting next to him or her. Meeting every Friday afternoon for a period of eight weeks, two school counselors gathered together a group of junior high school students who had lost a loved one to death within the last year.

One Friday afternoon, Sally shared with the group about her emotional reaction to her mom's death. She told her classmates about how she used to blame herself for her mother's death and how alone she felt without her mother. Herman dealt with his grief by getting into fights at school and at home with his older brother. He told the group about the four times he was sent to the principal's office in the month following his grandpa's death.

Ralph jumped in to tell the group about his inability to sleep at night, his restlessness, and his constant headaches. When it came time for Jasmine to share, she talked about how she was no longer interested in school or sports anymore, and about how she was unable to find a good reason to live after her best friend's suicide. Without her best friend, Jasmine felt like a nobody. The primary group facilitator then pointed out to the young people how each person's reaction to loss was different. Just as all the children were unique and special, so, too, were their reactions to the losses they had suffered.

The other group facilitator pointed out that for Sally, her comments reflected an emotional reaction to her mother's death, while Herman's words reflected a behavioral reaction to his grandpa's death. Ralph related several physical manifestations of grief, while Jasmine expressed changes in some of her cognitions since her friend's suicide. The facilitator was quick to remind students that everyone grieves in their own unique way. As several of them nodded their heads, the students seemed to grasp the notion that neither of their facilitators was going to force conformity onto the group nor would any one student try to "up" another student's story.

This commentary is a hypothetical description, but it shows when we interact with children we are likely to discover four different categories or types of grief. Grieving children who have lost a loved one to death, may respond to the loss on an emotional level, on a behavioral level, on a physical level, or on a cognitive level. Some children may even respond on several different levels at the same time! As each child is unique, no two children will experience the same manifestations of grief. Even twins can grieve in different ways.

Despite the unique nature of children's grief, there are a number of grief reactions, which are very common among grieving children. The remainder of this chapter will examine the four different types of grief reactions. Under each type of grief reaction there will be examples of various ways grief may manifest itself. It is important to remember that not all children will experience all of these grief reactions. Rather, these are examples of grief reactions that many grieving children have experienced following the death of someone loved. It is important to know that this is not an all-inclusive list. There are many other grief reactions besides those referred to in this chapter.

Emotional Reactions

We are aware of the fact that children's understanding of death differs according to each developmental stage. While very young children are not able to understand death as permanent, it is believed that they do experience some feelings such as sadness or protest when separated from their nurturing caretaker or parent. Therefore, the importance of supporting grieving children, especially young children, is more about their ability to feel, than it is about their ability to understand.

Denial And Numbness

While each child's grief is unique and individualized, in many cases after a death, denial is the first emotion that children feel. Because children do not want to hurt or be vulnerable, they often deny the death. Denial is the way children subconsciously block out painful information. By denying that their loved one has died, they can postpone and thereby hope to avoid all the unpleasantness and stress that accompanies death. It is almost as if children think that if they convince themselves that the death has not occurred, then it will not have actually occurred. "Willy didn't die. I know he wouldn't leave me like that."

In the first month or two following a death, children often perform their daily tasks as if their bodies are on "auto-pilot." While their bodies are going through the motions, they are not really aware of what is going on around them. Sometimes in the early stages of grief, children are so numb to what is going on around them that they are unable to connect what has been told to them with what they are actually feeling.

Perceived Lack Of Feelings

It is a very normal grief reaction for children to go off and play after being told about the death of a loved one. Adults often misinterpret this to mean that children either do not care or that they are not dealing with their feelings. Through play, children are embracing their pain the only way they know. Because the hurt and pain is more than they are able to handle at one time, children often resort to what they know best, namely playing, in order to pace themselves in their grief.

Anxiety And Fear

Following the death of a loved one, children may experience anxiety and fear in one to three different modes. If a parent or caretaker has died, it is normal for children to worry and encounter anxiety about who will now care for them. In this first mode, grieving children often feel abandoned and rejected when someone close to them dies. Since children are dependent on the adults around them, they often feel desperate and anxious about the future. For some children, this anxiety and fear can lead to despair.

Because small children are egocentric, they do not think of their parents or caretakers as people who have careers and commitments, which give meaning to their lives. Instead they only see their loved one's identity wrapped up in providing and caring for them. Henceforth, when those individuals die, some children take it personally and feel deserted.

When there has been a close relationship between a loved one and a surviving child, the death might feel like a loss of part of the self for the child. This is the second type of anxiety and fear that some children encounter when loved ones die. People are social by nature; when loved ones die, anxiety surfaces because children see themselves as part of their loved ones. Some children may unconsciously think, "Who am I now that Mommy is dead?"

As children reach early adolescence, they are becoming aware of the fact that death is universal and inevitable. Therefore, when a loved one dies, children who are nine years old and older are beginning to face the reality that they too will die one day. Along with this awareness of one's own mortality comes fear and anxiety. While life before was mostly fun and games, children now are beginning to confront that monumental reality, which causes great anxiety to many adults, namely, the reality that they will not live forever. This is a third way anxiety and fear can surface in grieving children.

Anger

Anger is one of the most common emotional reactions of grieving children. A parallel to grieving children experiencing anger is the reaction that takes place when a small child is lost in a large shopping mall. After thirty minutes of sobbing and frantically searching for his mother, six-year-old Colin ends up at the customer service booth where a security guard pages his mother. Instead of being happy when he is finally reunited with his mother, Colin protests and shows anger. Upon seeing his mother coming toward him, the boy does not initially hug his mother. Instead, he expresses anger at having been abandoned. Likewise, anger at a deceased loved one is a common manifestation of grief in children.

Not only will children express anger at their loved one for dying or abandoning them, but some children will express anger at other family members or themselves for not having done enough to keep their loved one alive. Being angry at doctors or at God is another grief reaction exhibited by children. Because of their feelings of powerlessness, anger is very common grief in children. Unfortunately adults often misinterpret anger as a bad behavior when it is actually a sincere and valid expression of a child's grief.

Yearning And Pining

"If only things were like they once were," said the little girl to her Uncle Wilhelm. "I wish we had our old life back before Adele and Aunt Gussie were killed by that drunk driver." Because small children operate with magical thinking and since cartoon characters show the power of wishes coming true, children often react to death by wishing things could return to the way they once were.

While some children yearn and pine for the return of their loved one due to their magical thinking and because television and cartoons reinforce that much of life can have a happy ending, at the same time other children yearn and pine for a reunion with a loved one simply as a result of their feelings of emptiness and deep sadness.

Searching

Closely related to yearning and pining is the grief reaction known as searching. Since small children have a difficult time understanding and accepting death as permanent, and because they do not want to give up on the possibility of a reunion with their loved one, some children may continue to search for their loved one in familiar places. In the years following a death, children may continue to look for their loved one when passing by Dad's old work place or when shopping in their little sister's favorite toy store. If the death occurred with unanswered questions, children may seek to find clues and investigate for years to come, in hopes that perhaps a mistake could have been made.

Guilt And Self-Blame

Despite efforts by adults and other family members to help children realize that the death was not their fault or that their actions did not cause the loved individual to die, children often still blame themselves and still feel guilty about their perceived role in the loss. Children often think that their words spoken in anger or their bad behaviors are able to inflict illness or even death upon other people. If a child had earlier wished that his little brother would die and later his younger sibling actually died, it would be a normal grief reaction for the older child to blame himself. If a child was constantly getting in trouble, she might think that her "being bad" caused Mommy to die.

In a support group for children, nine-year-old Dane told group members that he felt responsible for his mother's death. After getting permission, Dane's friend came over to play. He rang the doorbell. As Dane's mother came down the steps to answer the door, her back went out. To this nine-year-old, his mother's cancer started that day. "Her back went out," Dane told our group. "I got mad at myself. I began to think that it was all my fault. That started it."

Emptiness And Sadness

Children feel empty inside upon the loss of someone they are close to. This is because their sense of self is often directly connected with their relationship to the deceased. When loved ones die, children feel a real void in their lives. They often feel hollow inside. Along with their emptiness, there are accompanying feelings of sadness. While some children will cry and sob for great lengths of time, other children will withdraw from others and will not participate in anything that might bring joy or happiness into their presence.

When friends from church or from the neighborhood come to the home of people who have experienced the death of someone loved, the children often get ignored. When the adults are talking and listening to one another and grieving, children are being ignored or forgotten. This can make grieving children feel all the more alone and sad. Adults are often surprised to discover that feelings of emptiness and deep sadness are quite prevalent in grieving children.

Relief

Even though very few children or adults will ever admit that they feel relief following the death of a loved one who experienced tremendous suffering or was in a coma for a very long period, relief is a common grief reaction. Because watching a loved one suffer or linger is very difficult, some grieving children will experience feelings of relief after a loved one has breathed their last breath. While feeling a sense of relief, children may also experience sadness and loneliness at the same time.

Behavioral Reactions

Directly associated with their emotional reaction to death, children can respond behaviorally to their loss. While some adults may not be aware of what grieving children are feeling at a given time, it is rather difficult not to notice children expressing their grief through their actions and behaviors. We can learn a great deal about how children are embracing their grief by observing their conduct and mannerisms.

Aggressive And "Acting Out" Behavior

Following the death of a loved one, it is not uncommon for children to engage in fights and arguments and to be more loud and demanding than ever before. While children may have been quiet and well behaved prior to the death, following a loved one's death, children may begin to rebel against rules and may even change their friends at school. Children who once were obedient and dependable may become angry and hostile when asked a question or when told to perform a chore. When asked, "What do you want now?" the child may respond, "Why don't you just leave me alone?"

Sometimes children might skip school or lie to their parents about their whereabouts. Older children might act out their grief by engaging in behaviors such as drinking, using drugs, driving the car too fast, becoming sexually promiscuous, or possibly cutting themselves. Family members and caring adults need to be aware that while the early adolescent and adolescent years are very difficult, these difficult times can become more complicated when death enters into a child's world. Adults who live with or work with early adolescents and adolescents need to be mindful that "acting out" behavior is often not done to intentionally disrupt the family or one's community; rather, it frequently occurs when older children do not know how to handle their feelings and their pain.

Regressive Behavior

A normal manifestation of grief is for children to revert back to actions and behaviors they once engaged in when at an earlier developmental stage. Because they desire the security and comfort that came along with those earlier behaviors, grieving children often regress in their behaviors to an earlier time in their childhood. While some of these behaviors can be controlled, others are acted out unconsciously. Like children who are acting out, children who regress back to an earlier developmental stage need reassurance and comfort more than harsh discipline.

Upon the death of a loved one, small children may forget how to do things like tie their shoes or dress themselves. They may revert back to baby talk or may want to be held and rocked again. Some children might lose control of their bladder or bowels, despite the fact that they have been toilet trained several years earlier. Whining, thumb sucking, tantrums, desiring to sleep with parents again, and the constant wish to not be separated from their caregiver, are some of the regressive behaviors observed in grieving children.

Distraction And Hyperactivity

While many children already have a lot of energy and are constantly seeking things to do following a death, children are often hyperactive and desire to stay busy every waking moment. One of the reasons that grieving children want to keep busy is that they will not have to think about the death and the absence of their loved one. Instead of sitting idle, grieving children may constantly talk, sing, hum, fidget, or play with electronic gadgets or cell phones.

Often, children get involved in extracurricular activities at school or in the community so that they can keep their minds off their pain. Despite their activity and their busyness, when asked to talk about their activities, we often learn that children are not concentrating on what they are doing at all. Instead of focusing on the activity they are participating in, they may be distracted. In most cases, children who are grieving are not even consciously aware that they are trying to avoid their pain.

Disorganization

Because grieving takes so much energy, it is difficult for grieving children to focus on anything outside of their grief. It is a common grief reaction for children to show a decline in their school grades because they are temporarily unable to focus on their work. Staring out the window, doodling on a notebook, and constantly going over the details surrounding the death or death scene are some ways children respond to grief following the loss of someone they loved. Deciding what to wear to school or which restaurant to eat at when given several choices, may overwhelm or frustrate children who earlier could make decisions instantly. While children normally return to a better functioning level given time and support, family members and caring adults need to provide understanding and empathy during these hard times.

Withdrawal

Shying away from the crowd and avoiding friends is also a common grief reaction. When the pain is more than they can handle, instead of seeking out a friend to talk with, grieving children sometimes withdraw from others. This tendency to avoid relationships and contact with others is frequently made worse at school when classmates avoid grieving children for fear of saying the wrong thing. When avoidance by peers takes place, this makes hurting children feel more alone and isolated.

"Perfect" Child Or "Bad" Child Syndrome

Along the lines of acting out or aggressive behavior, some children's grief manifests itself in their becoming "bad children." Even if they were normally well-behaved and "good" before the death, some children may unconsciously become "bad" so that they can get the attention and care they so desperately need. Often children may not even be aware of their naughty or destructive behavior until someone points out just how horrible their behavior has become. In many cases, children are hurting so much that their negative actions are surfacing with little or no conscious thought given to them.

On the other hand, some children may go to the opposite extreme and become "perfect children," in an attempt to make their parents feel better or to receive affirmation from the caring adults around them. Upon the death of his younger brother, a ten-year-old child became the "perfect child." At the funeral of his younger sibling, the older brother took on the role of the surrogate spouse when his father was not attending to his wife. If the mother was left alone for a minute, the little boy would hurry to his mother's side and offer words of comfort.

When the casket was about to be closed in preparation for the funeral, the mother began to wail. Attempting to comfort his mother, the ten-year-old said, "Billy is okay. He is with Jesus now." Upon his return to school following his brother's funeral, the boy's parents worried about how he would do in school. They were concerned that like many grieving children, their son's performance and grades might drastically decline. However, once this boy returned to school, his grades skyrocketed and he brought home all A's. Because of his sensitivity to his parent's pain, this child was determined to please his parents in every way he could.

Avoiding Places Or
Things That Remind Them Of The Loved One

Wanting to stay away from Dad's office or avoiding places like the church or cemetery are common grief reactions. Many children who are grieving try as best they can to stay clear of those places or objects, which might remind them of their loved one and make them vulnerable to pain and hurt. Sometimes even seeing a piece of art that Grandpa painted or riding the bus by Mom's fitness club can instantly bring a child to tears. In some cases, children want to discard the deceased individual's clothing or personal objects immediately following a death so that they will not be constantly reminded of their loved one.

Keeping Objects Of The Deceased With Them Or
Visiting Places That Remind Them Of Their Loved One

Because every child is different and unique, there are other children who do not want to avoid reminders of their loved one, but want to keep their loved one's memory alive in every possible way. These children may want to wear clothing that belonged to their loved one, or they may want to walk by Aunt Lucy's house every day on the way home from school. By doing these things, they are attempting to keep their memories alive.

In a support group with children that I cofacilitated, a ten-year-old girl wore a laminated pin on her lapel that contained a picture of her little brother who had died two years earlier. When asked about her pain, she responded, "I feel better when I wear it."

Temporary Assumption Of The Personality Or
Role Of The Deceased

Without the deceased member of the family around anymore, grieving, children will often appoint themselves to take over the tasks of deceased individuals. For example, little girls may take over some of the roles of their mother like cooking or cleaning in order to "help out." Sometimes, boys feel that they must become "the man of the house" when their father or stepfather dies. Counselors and psychologists refer to this process as "role reorganization." Unfortunately, people in the community, and sometimes relatives, often force unwanted or inappropriate roles onto grieving children. Telling a twelve-year-old boy that he has to "take care" of his hurting mother in the future or a fourteen-year-old girl that it is her job now to help raise her little brothers because her mother has died are examples of poor behavior from outsiders.

Sometimes children will go so far as to take on the personality of deceased loved ones in an effort to replace the loved one or in an attempt to keep their memory alive. I learned from a congregation member that his six-year-old grandson began to talk like his deceased great-grandfather after the man's father had died. While the boy was not particularly close to his great-grandfather, after his death, the boy started liking the same foods his great-grandfather liked, began talking like the man used to, and began saying that he liked many of the same things as his deceased relative.

Physical Reactions

Encountering the emotional roller coaster and having to confront the myriad of behavioral changes are not the only types of grief reactions that we as caring adults need to be cognizant of with grieving children. Besides supporting children in these areas, family members and caring adults need to be aware of the many types of physical symptoms that may accompany grief.

Changes In Sleep Habits

It is very common for bereaved children to encounter changes in their sleeping routines. Some children, especially those who are sad and depressed, may want to sleep all the time. If someone does not wake them and make them get out of bed, these children may sleep the days away. On the other hand, many grieving children find it difficult to sleep after losing a loved one to death. Having trouble falling asleep at night is a normal grief reaction as is also waking up numerous times in the middle of the night.

A ten-year-old girl in a support group shared with group members that she still woke up regularly in the middle of the night and had difficulty returning to sleep. Her younger brother had died two years earlier, but she continued to have problems sleeping the night through.

Fear often plays a role in sleep difficulties for grieving children. Some children are fearful of dreaming about their loved one while others are fearful of sleeping alone in their room without their previous companion. Meanwhile, other grieving children may be afraid that they may not awake from sleep if a loved one died in their sleep. Other reasons for sleep disturbances may include preoccupation with the deceased, sadness, loneliness, anger, or guilt.

Changes In Eating Habits

Going out for pizza and frequenting their favorite fast-food restaurants might have once been a big event for children; however, following the death of a loved one, grieving children may now have very little appetite. It is a normal grief reaction for children who are grieving to lose their desire for food. Often grieving children will only pick at their food, and much of their previous excitement about a favorite dish or dessert will vanish when they are grieving.

While many grieving children respond to a death by losing their appetite, there are other children who indulge in food to the opposite extreme. Overeating, even to the point of almost being sick, may be how some children respond to their hurt and pain. This grief reaction is often nicknamed "stuffing one's feelings." Like some adults, there are some children who try to eat their pain away.

Other Physical Reactions

There are dozens of other physical symptoms that grieving children may experience following the death of someone loved. Some of the more common physical reactions to grief include the following: headaches, stomachaches, nausea, diarrhea, lack of muscular strength, fatigue, shortness of breath, tightness in the throat, dizziness, skin rashes, an increased number of colds and infections, changes in bladder and bowel habits, and more frequent allergic reactions.

The same child who told us in the children's grief group that she had trouble sleeping at night also claimed to suffer from stomachaches when she got to school every day. After hearing her story, we learned that she and her brother rode the bus together to school. Following his death, she was put on a new bus where she sat alone. She reported no stomach problems when at home, and we discovered from careful listening and a variety of questions that it was only at school that this physical symptom occurred.

Sometimes caring adults have to keep their antennas up in order to understand that some grief reactions may only be associated with specific triggers and circumstantial situations. Another important factor to be mindful of is to recognize that some physical symptoms will come and go. One moment, a child might be feeling completely healthy and be outdoors playing and laughing. Ten minutes later, that same child might come inside and report several physical symptoms, which are associated with grief.

When spending time with grieving children, be alert for the possibility of physical reactions returning during specific times of the year. Times of the year when families and caring adults might want to focus toward the reemergence of physical manifestations of grief in children might include the following: the anniversary of the death, holiday times, major events in the lives of grieving children, and when families customarily gather as a family unit.

Cognitive Reactions

The fourth and final type of grief reaction that grieving children experience, pertains to their thought patterns and cognitions. Cognitive reactions are often the most difficult to pick up on, because children are generally not able to articulate what is going on inside their heads. How children perceive what is going on around them, and even how they perceive themselves, is not something that most children are able to talk about in a clear and concise manner.

Reduction In Self-Esteem

When children have formed a close bond with someone, the death of that person often threatens a child's sense of self. If children have healthy attachments and good relationships with family members or close friends and one of them dies, the child's self-esteem may diminish due to the cessation of that relationship. With the death of a loved one, a child's sense of security is often greatly reduced. "Who can I count on now? He was the only one who really understood me."

In the case of sudden deaths and in some single-parent situations, family members may need to shuffle children around until a stable, suitable permanent place is found for the grieving children. When this happens, it is very difficult for children to find the type of support and care that they once knew and depended on.

It is not uncommon for children to rebel and act out in their new residential setting. In many cases, this pushes them even further away from the love and support that they so desperately need and crave. Some grieving children may completely withdraw from all social interaction and not be receptive to new relationships and new avenues for support and love. When these situations arise, children often feel bad about themselves and their self-esteem is greatly diminished. Some grieving children worry, "Will I ever be able to love and trust another person again? What is wrong with me?"

Confusion

"I can't remember what you told me to do this morning, Bill. What were those chores again?" the teenager asked his stepfather for the third time. Then as the boy went outside and began to rake the leaves in the yard, he could not remember what his stepfather had told him to do with the leaf piles. "What is it that I usually do with them?" he asked himself. He simply could not remember. Having difficulty remembering things and a lack of concentration are common grief reactions for grieving children. To grief-stricken children, confusion is more prevalent than clear thinking.

Preoccupation

While it is natural to think about the deceased constantly in the days and months following death, in some cases children will be preoccupied about their loved one for an extended period of time. Remembering every possible detail of times spent together, reflecting upon the last visit with the loved one, and constantly thinking about the loved one are some of the cognitive reactions children experience upon the death of someone loved.

In some cases, grieving children will hash out again and again possible ways to get their loved one back. Despite the attempts of caring adults in encouraging children to take a break and give themselves permission to have some fun for a little while, some children who are preoccupied have difficulty letting go of their fixation on the deceased.

Continued Avoidance And Denial Of The Death

In most cases of healthy grief, children will come to realize that they must face their pain and loss, and life must go on without their loved one. However, in some instances, children will continue to deny the death, and they will seek to avoid dealing with all the feelings and realities that accompany a death. Some grieving children report that they can still feel the presence of their loved one near them in certain situations. However, in some of these cases, this feeling of nearness may further prolong the child's denial.

Idealization Of The Past And/Or The Future

Sometimes when people die, the loved ones who are left behind look to the past with rose-colored glasses and fond memories. For children who have had positive relationships in the past and who have had healthy attachments, they may only remember the good times, thereby idealizing their pasts. While things certainly were not always perfect, these grieving children will find solace and comfort in recalling how great their lives used to be.

Meanwhile, other grieving children may place all their hope and confidence in the future trusting that things will greatly improve and get better in the days and months ahead. If children lived in a dysfunctional or unhealthy living environment, they may look to the future as an opportunity for all their dreams to come true and for all of their hurts and pains to disappear. Henceforth, they may idealize the future expecting that only good things can now come their way.

Increase In The Number Of Nightmares/Dreams

Another cognitive reaction to death is for children to experience more nightmares and dreams than they normally had before the death took place. Because grieving children have so much on their minds and because their bodies have experienced a number of physical symptoms since the death, children may have more dreams and nightmares than in the past.

If the dreams are good dreams, children may not mind going to sleep. However, if the dreams or nightmares are disturbing or scary, then children may be afraid to go to sleep. When children are afraid to go to sleep, the combination of the nightmares and the lack of sleep may further cloud their perceptions and thought patterns.

Changes In Spirituality

Children who are in the early adolescent to adolescent ages often experience changes in their spirituality when a death or other major loss takes place in their lives. When their parents separate and divorce, children often search for meaning in their lives. Likewise when events like a natural disaster takes place, when a fire destroys a home, or when a loved one dies, older children try to make sense out of what has happened.

When death or other losses take place in the lives of older children, some of these grieving children question where God is and why God allowed their loved one or their lost reality to be taken from them. Sometimes this spiritual questioning can lead to doubting or possibly a loss of belief in God.

On the other hand, some children grow closer to God when tragedy or death strikes. Some children find comfort in prayer and feel better by holding on to a belief that God is watching over them. Some children have articulated that while relatives and friends are sometimes too busy to talk to them and listen to them in the days and weeks after a death, they find it comforting to know that God is always there to listen to them. Henceforth, grieving children can react to a loss by either an increase in their spirituality or a decline in their spirituality. Again, it is important to remember that no two people grieve alike.

What Caring Adults Can Do To Help Children Embrace Their Grief

As people of faith, God exhorts his followers to build up one another and to love one another. When children are grieving as a result of the death of someone loved, the church family has an opportunity to extend their love and support to their younger brothers and sisters in Christ. When we extend our care to others, we are not doing so in order to earn merit or favor with God; rather, our benevolent actions are done in response to God's gracious love for us. Because God loves us and cares for us, we want to extend our love and our care to others. As children around us are hurting, there are a number of things that caring adults can do to assist them in their grief process.

Knowing that we cannot "fix" them or take their pain away, the first and most important thing caring adults can do for grieving children is to simply to be there for them. Walking with or companioning grieving children is a privilege that God makes available to many of his followers. Unfortunately, sometimes we are so busy with our lives that we do not realize the opportunity that has been placed before us. Notice that I am not describing this task as a burden, but rather as a privilege. Over the years, I have grown incredibly by being allowed to walk with hurting people. While death certainly changes the lives of those who are grieving, those of us who walk with grieving individuals find that we are changed by sharing the grief and the lives of others. Henceforth, if you chose to companion someone during their grief journey, be prepared for change and growth!

Those of you who are reading this book may fall into a variety of categories. You may be related to the child who is grieving. You may be a friend or a neighbor to the child. The child who is hurting may be a member of your congregation. You may be a pastor, a youth worker, a Christian educator, a member of the congregation's leadership team, or you may be a fellow worshiper who simply feels inclined to reach out to someone who is grieving.

In this chapter, I will be offering a number of "tips" or suggestions on how you might be able to help grieving children to embrace their grief following the death of someone loved. Like the chapter on grief reactions, this chapter is not all-inclusive. However, it is my hope that some of these suggestions or "tips" might be useful to you in your ministry with grieving children.

What I am proposing you follow is a model called a "ministry of presence" or a "compassionate presence." Your role is primarily "to be" with another person who is grieving. You are encouraged to show compassion, empathy, and acceptance. As adults know, children will be children. Sometimes they will do things or use language that we do not approve. As a caring adult who is companioning a child through grief, it is important to remember that your role is to love and support the child, even if you do not approve of or agree with some of the child's behaviors or actions. When children are hurting, they do not need to be berated or judged. While you can let them know that you may not always agree with or like what they do, you should assure them of your unconditional love and support.

Small children often worry about who will take care of them and love them after loved ones have died. As a caring adult, it might be useful to inform grieving children that you plan to be by their sides for a long time. When addressing security issues and fears of being abandoned, it might be beneficial for you to find ways to show hurting children that you are nearby whenever they might need you. Periodic phone calls or play dates might show grieving children that you plan to "practice what you preach." If the children are older, consider attending sporting events, musical performances, or functions in the community in which the children are participating. This will confirm your interest and support of them.

As was articulated earlier in this book, some grieving children blame themselves for the death of loved ones. Instead of dismissing or discounting their opinions and feelings, listen carefully to what the children are telling you. Let them know that you are really interested in why they feel that the death was their fault. Even if children continue to blame themselves, it is very important to allow grieving children to own their feelings. Remember the feelings are theirs and not yours. You have not walked in their shoes, even though you might genuinely want to understand what they are going through.

In many families, parents and relatives feel it is their duty to correct what they perceive to be wrong or false beliefs in their children. Your role as a caring adult is different. You may be the only person who actually gives a grieving child permission to express his or her innermost feelings. Consequently, you might be the one person who is given permission to enter the private and vulnerable world of a grieving child! Do not judge grieving children when they express their feelings. Allow children to express their anger, their guilt, and their feelings of blame. As hard as it might be, resist the inclination to "fix" their thinking.

When children ask questions that you do not know the answers to, encourage them to speak to people who might provide them with answers. Never discourage children from asking questions. Allow children to see you as a person who welcomes dialogue and questions. You may be the only person who is not shutting them down right now. Keep the communication lines open. Let them see that you are a person who can be trusted and depended upon.

As children begin to express their deepest feelings either through their words or through their play, never react in shock or disgust. If children sense you are shocked by their words or are judging them, they will shut down communication. Try to be an empathetic listener whose agenda is not your own but the child's. Always put the feelings and the needs of the grieving child before your own. If you later feel that you need to process what you are feeling or if you are grieving the loss of the same person, find a trustworthy friend and share your feelings with him or her. However, do not place grieving children in the position of their having to take care of your emotional needs. You are there to support them in the midst of their brokenness and pain and not vice versa.

Do not pity grieving children by repeatedly telling them that you feel sorry for them. Instead, share their grief and allow them to lean on you emotionally. Be an empathetic listener who shares their pain by providing validation and understanding. Use what is called "mirroring techniques" when applicable. This is a technique where the listener summarizes or "mirrors" what he or she has just heard. Mirroring is essentially paraphrasing what you heard someone say.

Perhaps fifteen-year-old Mary Catherine has just told you how hard things have been for her since her older brother, George, died during a prank at his college fraternity house. "Nobody realizes that I miss George, too. Everybody is giving Mom and Dad all the attention. Not one person has told me what a good sister I was to George. I was his sister for fifteen years. Doesn't that count for anything?"

As the caring adult, you want to let Mary Catherine know that you have heard what she said. Since she perceives that no one is validating her grief, it is crucial that Mary Catherine hear that you heard her express her feelings of pain and sadness. You might mirror what she said by the following: "Mary Catherine, you are feeling that people are ignoring you and your grief. Your parents are getting all the attention and you feel left out. You miss George, too. Did I get that right?" By closing your comments with a question, this might open the door for further dialogue.

Earlier in this book, I talked about how some people use euphemisms when they are at a loss for words. When people see friends, relatives, or members of their church family in pain, the immediate reaction is often to say or do something to take the pain away. Instead of stating a euphemism, consider putting your arm around a grieving individual and give him or her a hug. Sometimes simply encouraging the person to cry if tears have formed in their eyes is helpful. Other times sitting next to a person who is crying and simply being with them shows your care and your Christian love.

Avoid quoting scripture as a means of comfort. While many Christians look to the Bible as a great means of comfort and inspiration, quoting verses of scripture to grieving children is usually not very helpful. Even if children are old enough to believe in heaven or the promise of resurrected life, that theological belief usually does not alleviate or reduce their feelings of sadness or loneliness for the person who has died.

When my father's funeral was conducted following his brief battle with cancer, I can recall very vividly how eloquently one of the pastors preached about the promise of the resurrection. Even though the pastor's words were eloquent and theologically very hopeful, I still cried throughout the service because I was missing my father. I was happy that Dad had been received into the arms of God's mercy, but I was sad that I no longer would have my father around to share my life. In other words, words of scripture can be comforting, but that does not mean that grieving individuals will stop missing their loved ones.

When the children are smaller and are not able to put their feelings into words, spend time playing with them instead. Play is how children express what is going on inside of them. When children are angry about something, this often will surface during their play. Likewise, when children are sad, this is often portrayed in their drawings, puppet shows, or in their Play-Doh creations. Invite children to teach you what they are feeling by becoming their playmates. When working with early adolescents or adolescents ask them to share their favorite music with you. What musical groups do they like? What sports teams do they follow? If they are interested in art, ask them if you can see their drawings or paintings. If they are learning to play the guitar, invite them to play some selections for you.

Use whatever opening grieving children give you and let them lead you into their world. Trust that some children will allow you into their space if they feel you are genuinely concerned about them. If they feel that you are merely being nosy or that you are only spending time with them because a family member has asked you to do so, you will probably not get very far. Children, like pets, are often very good judges of character and motive.

Remember special days in the lives of grieving children. The one-year anniversary of the death is often very difficult for people who are bereaved. The first Thanksgiving or Christmas without a loved one is usually quite hard. When a parent has died, recall how difficult Mother's Day or Father's Day might be for them. Is there some way you can let hurting children know that you care for them on this special day? Similarly, certain school events are difficult for children when parents are expected to attend and a parent has died. It is also important that you name the person that has died and allow children to talk about their loved ones. Thinking that others have forgotten their loved ones is very painful for many grievers.

When eleven-year-old Billy was invited to his first father-son Boy Scout campout after his dad's death, Billy began to withdraw from others. Because his mother was overwhelmed with trying to make ends meet and addressing her own grief, she had no idea why Billy was becoming reclusive. One Sunday night, the youth leader from Billy's church invited Billy to go out to a local batting cage with him. After hitting several rounds of balls and eating a hot fudge sundae, Billy opened up to his youth leader.

Billy admitted that he was feeling angry about his father's death, and his anticipation of the upcoming Boy Scout campout made him realize the permanence of his loss. Never again would he and his father do "guy things." Not knowing what to say or do, the youth leader admitted his inability to fix things. He said, "Billy, no one can bring your father back. None of us can replace him or take over the role of being your dad. But I'd like to ask you what I can do for you as your friend. Are there things church members and I can do for and with you to let you know we are here for you?" Billy quickly replied, "Nope." After a few seconds of awkward silence Billy blurted out, "Well, bringing me here once in a while might be cool. Before tonight, I had not touched a baseball since Dad's accident. So, if it's not too much to ask, could we come back here again sometime?"

Adult children who have lost loved ones to death will tell you that losing a parent is a loss that most of us are not truly prepared for. Since we have never known life without them, when a parent is gone from our lives we often do not know how to act. To not have parents attend special functions and celebrations of our success is very difficult for children regardless of their age. When a child gets a diploma, a trophy, or some special recognition, the absence of an important person in their lives will offer trigger grief. Caring adults need to be aware of this and make sure that someone special is present to accompany children for special events like banquets, award ceremonies, tournaments, or concerts.

Lastly and most importantly, pray for grieving children. Ask God to embrace those who are hurting and to comfort them in his tender care. Ask God to guide you and to help you as you walk with some of your younger brothers and sisters in Christ.

How Our Beliefs
Impact Our Grief

When death touches the lives of children, we, as adult Christians, have an opportunity to share our religious beliefs with our younger brothers and sisters. I do not mean that we should use death as a time to proselytize nonbelievers or to force our beliefs onto those who are vulnerable or broken. On the other hand, when death touches children or others around us, this may open a door for us to share how our Christian beliefs have brought us comfort and solace during our difficult times in life. Even though we may be feeling great sadness and emptiness when someone we loved has died, our trust and hope in the promise of the resurrection simultaneously brings us comfort and consolation.

One of the first things that many adults and children do when someone dies suddenly or unexpectedly is blame God. When people previously held to a belief in the goodness or the sovereignty of God, it sometimes comes into question whether someone or something treasured has been taken or removed from them. When the terrorist attacks took place in the eastern United States on September 11, 2001, many people began to ask the question, "Where is God?" Likewise, when parents divorce, a classmate is killed in a car accident, or a fire destroys a family's home and all the family's pets die, children sometimes wonder how God could allow this to happen.

From previous experience, many of us know that there is no easy way to answer or address these kinds of questions or concerns. You cannot simply and assuredly state that you know that God does not cause bad things to happen to good or undeserving people. In regard to a child's specific situation, you are certainly not capable of discerning what God did or did not do because you are not God. Like Job learned, none of us are the Creator, therefore we cannot know or understand all things as God our Creator does. In regard to getting answers to their questions, you may want to tell children that over the years a number of your questions have not been answered, either. Some things in life simply do not make sense.

While it is certainly okay and understandable that people might be angry with God when loved ones die or when we do not understand what is going on, it is helpful to let children know that anger is a very normal grief reaction. Many religious people have felt angry at God throughout history. Nothing is wrong with venting our anger toward God. Nor is anything wrong with being furious about what has happened to us as long as we do not harm ourselves or others when letting our anger out. Perhaps you might ask grieving children to come up with some possible ways to express their anger. Some children find that exercising, playing games, listening to music, journaling, hitting a punching bag, and so on can be useful ways to ventilate anger.

As a caring adult who has many years of life experience, one of the things you can do for grieving children is to share your beliefs with them. You might inform children that your life experience has helped you to see many of God's attributes. One of God's attributes is God's loving presence. You might tell grieving children about how God helped you following a difficult time in your life. When you could not muster enough strength to get out of the bed on many mornings following the death of your beloved grandparent, you believe that it was purely the grace of God that helped to rouse you out of bed. When you thought that you did not have the energy to push the lawn mower, somehow the grass managed to still get mowed.

God may also have served as your fortress and your foundation when everything else in life was seemingly crumbling before your eyes. Your faith in God may have been the only thing in your life that felt stable and secure. In this scenario, another of God's attributes is God's strength and dependability.

For those of us who are part of a Christian community where holy communion is frequently shared, sharing how God's means of grace strengthens you might be in order. One Sunday after learning that my father was dying from lung cancer, I can recall quite vividly that as the pastor placed the communion wafer in my hand, I felt God's presence in my life in a way that words cannot express.

Then, as I drank the communion wine, tears came into my eyes. At that vulnerable and painful time in my life, I trusted with every ounce of my being that God was really present with me. I was not alone. God was present with me in the form of bread and wine, and God continued to be with me every day during my father's illness and in the days and months of my grief which followed. This is yet another example of the loving presence of God, which is more commonly referred to theologically as the "real presence" of Christ.

As a parish pastor, countless numbers of people have talked to me over the years about how the love and care of other human beings helped them get through their difficult days. Many of these Christian believers told me that they were of the opinion that it was God who had provided people in their lives to feed them, to companion them through their darkest days, and to shower them with Christian love and care. While God was feeding them one moment at his altar in worship, the next moment, God had empowered other believers to nurture them with home-cooked meals and big teddy-bear hugs.

There are many examples that could be shared here, which illustrate how grieving individuals have found assistance in embracing their grief over the years following the death of a loved one. As the caring adults in your community, the question now arises, "How can you become the witness of Christ's love for a grieving child? How can you help hurting children to know that you care for them and that you are an extension of our loving God?"

Caring adults are reminded here that using euphemisms that blame God or connect God to the death should be avoided at all costs. Children are often confused when a loved one has died. When in doubt about what to say, remember the slogan, "Silence is golden." Avoid quoting a bunch of euphemisms when there is a lull in the conversation. Keep in mind that yours is a "ministry of presence" or a "compassionate presence." In many instances your simply being with grieving children is more important than what you say.

At some point in your relationship with grieving children, they may ask you about your faith. They may ask what you believe happens when someone dies. There may also be occasions when you are teaching a class at church or leading a youth group session and the topic of heaven or resurrection arises. These are wonderful opportunities for you to share your faith with others and perhaps offer hope to another believer.

While I have talked to hundreds of people over the years about their beliefs in the afterlife and what happens after physical death, a handful of those individuals discounted the validity of grievers continuing to express their grief because of their belief in the promise of eternal life. Likewise, I have heard several Christians tell others that because of their belief in eternal life, or heaven, and because of their certainty that their loved one now is with God that grievers should no longer feel sadness or grief. It is almost as if they are of the opinion that if a person believes in the resurrection, that means that relatives and close friends should not experience grief.

As a grief specialist and a minister, I completely disagree with this type of thinking. While we certainly find comfort and hope in the promises of a new life with God after our physical deaths, it is very normal and healthy to miss our loved one who has died. When you stop and think about it, we are not grieving for the person who has died, we are grieving for ourselves and our loss. Our loved one has been received into the arms of God's mercy; however, we are the ones remaining here on earth without them. Grief reactions like sadness, loneliness, emptiness, and confusion are not only normal, but also expected. What I am advocating here is the likelihood of ambiguity. Some grieving individuals may feel joy and happiness for the person who has died as a result of their theological beliefs. On the other hand, these same grievers may also be experiencing grief because they miss their loved ones.

While adults sometimes have a hard time balancing these two positions, one can imagine how confusing this must be for grieving children. As caring adults, you must tread gently here. It is important to keep in mind the developmental level of the children who are grieving. How you talk to a thirteen-year-old will vary greatly from how you talk to a five-year-old.

This brings us to that topic that most books about children and grief avoid, and that is how to talk to children about the afterlife.

How does one share something so personal as one's belief in heaven with grieving children?

One's beliefs in the afterlife are often very personal and private. On the other hand, as Christians, we are reminded that we are a community of believers — we are the body of Christ. Therefore, our faith is something which is communal. The apostle Paul repeatedly reminds his brothers and sisters in Corinth that "the body does not consist of one member but of many" (1 Corinthians 12:14).

In order to talk with grieving children about our faith, it is important that we as caring adults have a firm grasp on what we believe. It is especially significant that we have a fairly clear understanding of what we believe happens when a person dies. If we are uncertain or "wishy-washy" about what we believe, this may confuse children who are looking to us for guidance or possibly hope.

Many children are not able to comprehend most religious concepts until around the age of nine or ten. Keep in mind, however, that this is a general number. Some children have more cognitive abilities at earlier ages than others. Regardless of the age of children, most grieving children are intuitive enough to know when adults are telling them something that they do not truly believe in. Even though some children are not desiring a theological treatise when they ask us, "What happens when someone dies?" it is important that we are clear about what it is that we really believe. Also keep in mind that talking over children's heads will not help them understand the role our faith has in our lives.

Jesus loved little children and always welcomed them in his midst. As adult members of the body of Christ, we are called to love, to embrace, and to comfort them. In Matthew's gospel, Jesus talks to his disciples about children and true greatness. "Whoever welcomes one such child in my name welcomes me" (Matthew 18:5).

As Christian believers, we believe that Jesus Christ is victorious over sin and death. On the cross, Christ died so that we might live forever with him. We trust that physical death is not the end; rather, in our baptisms, we have been promised that we will be "like" Christ and "with" Christ forever. Chapter 15 of 1 Corinthians is a very helpful chapter to read regarding the resurrection of the dead as are many of Paul's other writings.

As Christians we trust that when we die, both our body and soul die. When we are raised to new life in Christ we are promised that we are changed. We are made new. And this new life is so much better and greater than anything we have ever experienced before on earth. Unlike Greek philosophy, which claims that there is an immortal soul which lives on, as Christians, we believe that once we die something totally new is being worked out in the resurrection. We can hardly even use our old, familiar language to speak about this new creation by God.

Paul writes about this new life in 1 Corinthians.

> *Listen, I will tell you a mystery! We will not all die, but we will all be changed, in a moment, in the twinkling of an eye, at the last trumpet. For the trumpet will sound, and the dead will be raised imperishable, and we will be changed.* — 1 Corinthians 15:51-52

When someone we love dies, we can also find comfort and hope in those familiar words from the Apostles' Creed: "I believe in the resurrection of the body and the life everlasting. Amen."

As you reach out to your younger brothers and sisters in Christ and assist them in embracing their grief, be forewarned that you will most likely encounter people who will disagree with your honest and straightforward approach to grieving children. There are many people who think that children should be protected at all costs, and death should be hidden from children. There will be people who will say that since you are not relatives that you are stepping into territory which does not belong to you. And, there will be people who think that you have no right to share your Christian beliefs with another — especially a vulnerable child. Recall that your actions are not being done to glorify yourself; rather, you are ministering to another in the name of Jesus Christ. You are God's hands at work in the community.

As God's children, claimed in the waters of holy baptism, I commend you for taking the time to read this book and to consider ways that you might extend your Christian love and care for others. It is my hope that you are now better equipped to teach children about death and to love and support them when they are grieving the death of a loved one. As fellow members of the body of Christ, I leave this quotation for you to ponder. "For where two or three are gathered in my name, I am there among them" (Matthew 18:20).

9 780788 025051